MW00423760

············ **HOW TO** ············

Open & Operate a
Financially Successful
Staffing
Service Business

With Companion CD-ROM

Kristie Lorette

How to Open & Operate a Financially Successful Staffing Service Business: With Companion CD-ROM

Copyright © 2012 by Atlantic Publishing Group, Inc.
1405 SW 6th Ave. • Ocala, Florida 34471 • Phone: 800-814-1132 • Fax: 352-622-1875
Website: www.atlantic-pub.com • E-mail: sales@atlantic-pub.com
SAN Number: 268-1250

No part of this publication may be reproduced, stored in a retrieval system, or transmitted in any form or by any means, electronic, mechanical, photocopying, recording, scanning, or otherwise, except as permitted under Section 107 or 108 of the 1976 United States Copyright Act, without the prior written permission of the Publisher. Requests to the Publisher for permission should be sent to Atlantic Publishing Group, Inc., 1405 SW 6th Ave., Ocala, Florida 34471.

Library of Congress Cataloging-in-Publication Data

Lorette, Kristie.
  How to open & operate a financially successful staffing service business : with companion CD-ROM / by Kristie Lorette.
     p. cm.
  Includes bibliographical references and index.
  ISBN-13: 978-1-60138-282-5 (alk. paper)
  ISBN-10: 1-60138-282-0 (alk. paper)
  1. Personnel management. 2. New business enterprises--Management. I. Title. II. Title: How to open and operate a financially successful staffing service business.
  HF5549.L5777 2011
  331.12'80681--dc23
                        2011029434

LIMIT OF LIABILITY/DISCLAIMER OF WARRANTY: The publisher and the author make no representations or warranties with respect to the accuracy or completeness of the contents of this work and specifically disclaim all warranties, including without limitation warranties of fitness for a particular purpose. No warranty may be created or extended by sales or promotional materials. The advice and strategies contained herein may not be suitable for every situation. This work is sold with the understanding that the publisher is not engaged in rendering legal, accounting, or other professional services. If professional assistance is required, the services of a competent professional should be sought. Neither the publisher nor the author shall be liable for damages arising herefrom. The fact that an organization or website is referred to in this work as a citation and/or a potential source of further information does not mean that the author or the publisher endorses the information the organization or website may provide or recommendations it may make. Further, readers should be aware that Internet websites listed in this work may have changed or disappeared between when this work was written and when it is read.

TRADEMARK DISCLAIMER: All trademarks, trade names, or logos mentioned or used are the property of their respective owners and are used only to directly describe the products being provided. Every effort has been made to properly capitalize, punctuate, identify, and attribute trademarks and trade names to their respective owners, including the use of ® and ™ wherever possible and practical. Atlantic Publishing Group, Inc. is not a partner, affiliate, or licensee with the holders of said trademarks.

Printed in the United States

PROJECT MANAGER: Gretchen Pressley • gpressley@atlantic-pub.com
BOOK PRODUCTION DESIGN: T.L. Price • design@tlpricefreelance.com
PROOFREADER: Andrell Bower • bowera@gmail.com
FRONT COVER DESIGN: Meg Buchner • megadesn@mchsi.com
BACK COVER DESIGN: Jackie Miller • millerjackiej@gmail.com

Printed on Recycled Paper

A few years back we lost our beloved pet dog Bear, who was not only our best and dearest friend but also the "Vice President of Sunshine" here at Atlantic Publishing. He did not receive a salary but worked tirelessly 24 hours a day to please his parents.

Bear was a rescue dog who turned around and showered myself, my wife, Sherri, his grandparents Jean, Bob, and Nancy, and every person and animal he met (well, maybe not rabbits) with friendship and love. He made a lot of people smile every day.

We wanted you to know a portion of the profits of this book will be donated in Bear's memory to local animal shelters, parks, conservation organizations, and other individuals and nonprofit organizations in need of assistance.

– *Douglas & Sherri Brown*

PS: We have since adopted two more rescue dogs: first Scout, and the following year, Ginger. They were both mixed golden retrievers who needed a home.

Want to help animals and the world? Here are a dozen easy suggestions you and your family can implement today:

- *Adopt and rescue a pet from a local shelter.*
- *Support local and no-kill animal shelters.*
- *Plant a tree to honor someone you love.*
- *Be a developer — put up some birdhouses.*
- *Buy live, potted Christmas trees and replant them.*
- *Make sure you spend time with your animals each day.*
- *Save natural resources by recycling and buying recycled products.*
- *Drink tap water, or filter your own water at home.*
- *Whenever possible, limit your use of or do not use pesticides.*
- *If you eat seafood, make sustainable choices.*
- *Support your local farmers market.*
- *Get outside. Visit a park, volunteer, walk your dog, or ride your bike.*

Five years ago, Atlantic Publishing signed the Green Press Initiative. These guidelines promote environmentally friendly practices, such as using recycled stock and vegetable-based inks, avoiding waste, choosing energy-efficient resources, and promoting a no-pulping policy. We now use 100-percent recycled stock on all our books. The results: in one year, switching to post-consumer recycled stock saved 24 mature trees, 5,000 gallons of water, the equivalent of the total energy used for one home in a year, and the equivalent of the greenhouse gases from one car driven for a year.

Table of Contents

Chapter 6: Financing 121

Chapter 7: Legal Concerns 157

Chapter 8: Insurance.............................165

Chapter 9: Hiring Employees 171

Chapter 10: Money Management............193

Chapter 11: Organization of the Office ... 209

Chapter 12: Advertising the Modern Way 223

Chapter 13: When You Want to Exit the Business — or Retire 259

Introduction

Once thought of as glorified employment agencies for temporary employees and administrative staff, staffing agencies place various types of employees with different types of companies. Today's staffing services offer variety and sophistication and provide employers with staff. Whether a company is hesitant to hire employees during a recession or desperate to fill openings during an expansion, the staffing industry provides professional help fulfilling these needs.

Some form of a staffing agency has existed as far back as human history can record. The way these agencies looked and matched employees with employers is different from what we would consider a staffing service today. Although staffing services have evolved during the last 30 years, the staffing industry makes $61.8 billion per year.

This book will help you decide whether a staffing service business is right for you. You need more than an entrepreneurial spirit and a good attitude to start and run a financially successful staffing service.

Each chapter of the book will walk you through the areas you should evaluate and the necessary steps to take before, during, and after launching your business. The book will also point out the pitfalls to avoid. You will find an analysis of the different types of staffing services and the specific requirements for each type. The case studies throughout the book help highlight and illustrate the topics each chapter covers in detail. The CD-ROM that comes with the book includes sample forms, schedules appropriate for a staffing service, and a sample business plan.

Starting and running a successful staffing service requires you to take in so much information. First, read the book from beginning to end without taking action on any of the steps. Absorb the information and let it soak in. Reading from beginning to end will also allow you to simultaneously get big-picture and detailed views of the staffing business. Go back through and read the sections of the book for a second time. Implement the steps, complete the worksheets, and complete the tasks to start and run your own staffing service business.

1

Staffing Services — What is It?

In essence, a staffing service is an employer, a business, and a contractor. Staffing services hire employees, pay those employees, withhold taxes from employee compensation, and offer employees benefits. Staffing services take on a business role because they provide a service to their clients. In this case, the service is providing employees, and the clients are the businesses or companies that contract the staffing service to find these employees on their behalf. Finally, staffing services are contractors because they act as a matchmaking service between employees and clients.

The Four Types of Staffing Services

The types of services these agencies provide fall into one of four main areas: administration, temporary services, contract employees, and executive recruitment. A staffing service focuses its efforts on one of the four niche areas rather than tries to be a generalist agency. Subcategories or subniches also emerge under each of the four primary categories. For example, if a staffing service specializes in executive recruiting, the agency might also specialize in a particular industry, such as the financial services industry. Although none of the categories are hard and fast, choosing one of the four primary categories is a starting point for deciding how to build the foundation for your staffing service.

The bottom line, and something that all the different types of staffing services have in common, is that the staffing agencies employ the individuals and place their employees in positions with their clients. Therefore, the staffing agency is still responsible for payroll and taxes for the employee even while the employee is placed within a company. However, services providing executive and administrative recruiting tend to place full-time, permanent employees with their clients. Once the employee begins working for companies in this situation, the individual becomes an employee of the client company, which is responsible for payroll and benefits.

Administrative

An administrative staffing service contracts with companies or businesses that have staffing needs but tends to concentrate on support positions rather than mid- to upper-level management and executive positions. The businesses or companies are the clients of the staffing agency; the staffing agency is not entering into a contract with the employee. The staffing service searches for and identifies individuals who fill the needs of the companies. The agency is simply acting as a matchmaker or liaison between the company and the employee. Employees that these types of agencies place tend to be long-term and full-time. In some situations, administrative staffing agencies also place part-time employees.

The "temp" agency

A temp agency provides temporary employees to companies. In this situation, the temporary worker becomes an employee of the staffing agency, which makes the staffing service responsible for employer-related activities. The staffing agency then places individuals into temporary positions with one of the agency's client companies. Temporary employees might fulfill a time period with one company for one week, one month, or one year before moving on to the next job where they are needed in the marketplace. In some cases, a temporary position has the ability to turn into a permanent position. In these situations, companies like to try employees out before offering them a full-time, permanent position with the company. According to the American Staffing Association (ASA), during a one-year period, staffing services have about 9.7 million individuals either with temporary or contract work. Of the 9.7 million, about 7 million make the transition into permanent job positions.

Contract employees

The third niche for staffing services is for contract employees. Contract employees are similar to temporary employees in that the contract for employment is for a set period of time. The primary difference is the contract employees have a written contract that both the employer and employee are bound to abide by. In the majority of circumstances, these positions are in human resources or payroll services. However, other types of positions are also included in this category of staffing services work.

CASE STUDY: EXPANDING AND GROWING SERVICE OFFERINGS

Lynda Zugec, Founder
The Workforce Consultants
14 West Park Court
Grand Island, NY 14072
(646) 797-2946
www.theworkforceconsultants.com

The Workforce Consultants operates as a corporation that specializes in placing contract employees. The company did not start by offering a staffing service, however. Including staffing as part of its offerings was a natural extension of human resources consultation. When the staffing service option started, The Workforce Consultants recognized an unfulfilled need in the marketplace. With the technology the firm had available, it was able to fill these needs faster and easier than competitors or startups.

Lynda Zugec runs the business from wherever her work takes her. To operate the staffing service, she only requires a computer and access to the Internet whether she is in North America, Europe, the Middle East, Asia, or somewhere in between.

The Workforce Consultants chose a virtual office because of its flexibility. Virtual businesses allow for a quick response time to satisfy client needs more efficiently and effectively than some other types of office structures. Zugec said the major disadvantage of running a virtual staffing service is clients and candidates sometimes have a hard time comprehending what a virtual business is and how it works. Zugec says it can be a challenge at times to explain the concept to them and make them feel comfortable in working with her on a virtual basis. She says it takes patience to explain that virtual, not face to face, meetings do not sacrifice the level of service the client receives.

Executive recruiting

The final category for staffing services is executive recruiting. Executive recruiting only deals with individuals who are at executive levels. Generally, these are employees who start at management level or higher. An offshoot of executive recruiting is **headhunting**, in which the recruiter uses his or her knowledge of a particular industry to find suitable candidates for a particular job. For example, if an executive recruiter specializes in marketing, he or she will have a pool of marketing professionals from which to find the right person for the position a company needs to fill. Executive recruiters who specialize in a particular job function or industry might recruit and place candidates at different levels, including those above and below management or executive levels.

Why Do People Start Staffing Service Businesses?

The people who start staffing services are often those who have worked for a staffing agency and want to branch out on their own. This is not always the case. Regardless of whether you have experience working in staffing, successful staffing service business owners possess entrepreneurial and managerial talents. Essentially, you need the education and experience to understand the work you are undertaking: matching people with the companies that need them to run. You also need to know how to use computers and software programs that make staffing work possible.

Keep in mind the four primary categories often overlap. A staffing service might find itself catering to a particular market, but as that market grows and changes, so does the opportunity to grow and expand its service offering. The market might even move your staffing service in an entirely new direction. During the past 30 years, staffing services in tune with the markets they serve have proved to be recession-proof businesses. Clients who are reluctant to hire new employees in a recession tend to turn to staffing agencies to fill their needs. Booming agencies tend to be those that can find suitable employees who fit the needs of their clients no matter what the economic or unemployment situation.

Managerial talent is also an important characteristic of someone who runs a successful staffing service. Running a staffing agency is all about being able to read and manage people. Staffing is, after all, a people business. You have to be able to analyze experience on a piece of paper or application and match it with the criteria employers are seeking. You need to be able to interview someone and get to know them well enough to identify whether they are the right person for the job. You also need the ability to motivate others, counsel them to show up to work on time and do what they are supposed to do, and manage the relationship between the company and the employees you place there.

Who Uses Staffing Services?

The people who use staffing services run the gamut. They might be large corporate companies with a sudden vacancy or those that need to put individuals on a new project. Other companies might need employees but do not want to handle the requirements that come with having their own set of permanent employees. You might even cater to sole proprietors or small business owners who have an occasional need for staff. Generally, companies that reach out for the help of a staffing agency fall into one of four primary categories: those in emergency situations, companies that do not need permanent employees, businesses with seasonal or occasional needs, and companies with special projects or a temporary need for help.

The emergencies

Emergencies tend to occur because an unexpected situation arises. Emergencies in a business can range from a pivotal employee leaving the firm to operating in the aftermath of a natural disaster. Whether the need is to replace someone who has left the company or to bring on an extra person or two to complete work over a short period of time, after emergency situations, hiring companies tend to turn to a staffing agency. A staffing agency can help the companies and businesses to quickly respond to the emergency and last-minute needs as quickly and efficiently as possible.

No permanent employees

Some businesses, organizations, and companies do not want permanent employees on their payroll. Following employment practices, managing payroll services, providing benefits, and a myriad of other activities come along with being an employer. Rather than having to deal with the day-to-day burdens that the employer role can bring, some organizations turn to temporary employment agencies for their ability to manage the services that go along with employing. This prevents the company from having to manage employees and instead leaves the human resources side of doing business to the staffing agency.

Occasional need for help

Businesses grow and change. When this happens, they might need to bring more employees on to the staff. This is especially true of seasonal or cyclical businesses or industries. During peak times, some companies turn to staffing agencies for help finding employees to fill their occasional needs. For example, a gift distributor might have longer work hours during the holiday season than other times of the year. During the holidays, the company brings on additional administrative staff and customer service representatives to help it deal with the higher demand for its products. After the holiday season is over, the gift distributor might retain some additional staff to manage an influx of returns or refunds, but after the holiday rush is over, it no longer requires the extra employees.

Special projects or needs

Any business that has a temporary or project-based need for help often turns to staffing services for help fulfilling its needs. For example, when a law firm is working on a big case, it will bring in extra workers to make copies, run errands for the attorneys on the case, and bring in lunch for the associates and attorneys working the case. An accounting firm might bring in temporary employees to field the high volume of phone calls and make copies of tax documents that increase leading up to tax time. An event planner running a large conference or trade show brings on additional administrative staff during the planning and implementation. Once the trade show is over, the special project need is gone, and so are the employees.

Although four primary categories or needs cause businesses to turn to staffing services, they also overlap. Generally, opportunities tend to arise as the business grows. To find qualified and professional employees, staffing services tend to have a pool of candidates they can pull from to help companies fill their needs. They also tend to have the experience and knowledge required to find, identify, interview, and place the best possible people for the position or positions the company is trying to fill. Business owners and managers who change as the market changes understand the value of quality employees and understand the value of the human resources management staffing services provide.

The reasons companies turn to staffing services to help them identify employees vary. One of the primary reasons companies hire staffing services is they have not been able to find and fill positions with individuals who fit the qualifications the companies seek. When a company has exhausted its own recruiting efforts, it might turn to staffing services to take over the search and recruitment process.

Are Staffing Services Recession-Proof?

When you consider that historical records indicate some form of staffing services has been in existence since the 14th century in Germany and the first known U.S. staffing service began in Boston in 1848, it is easy to believe staffing services can take the ups and downs in the economy. Considering that the modern recruiting or staffing service started in 1926 and has continued to flourish as an industry, you can believe it is an industry that is here to stay in some form.

According to the U.S. Bureau of Labor Statistics, the category that recruiting and staffing falls under, management consulting, is the largest-growing industry in the country. The future employment outlook also demonstrates the need for staffing services to help with the expected shortage of qualified candidates needed to fulfill the positions of the 78 million baby boomers who are retired or heading toward retirement. With only 49 million of the Generation X population to fill these jobs, the employee shortage is roughly 29 million qualified individuals.

The huge increase in unemployment that followed the downturn in the economy that began at the end of 2007 somewhat affects these figures. Despite the Great Recession, the outlook for the need of staffing services is still high. During times of high unemployment or hard economic times, companies have difficulty finding qualified employees to fill the open positions they have available in their companies.

The reason for this is twofold. First, staffing is not just about putting warm bodies into a position or job. Running a staffing service is about putting the best and most qualified person in the job or position. Staffing service professionals should have the experience and knowledge to find and place these candidates for their clients. Second, some industries continue to grow despite the economic situation. Health care is one example. A myriad of health care professionals, including nurses, doctors, dental hygienists, and medical coders, are in demand. The legal field also seems to be a recession-proof industry that is continuously growing and hiring.

No matter which focus you take for your staffing services, there are businesses, industries, and organizations out there that need the services you will provide. Most staffing agencies focus their efforts in some way, whether by specializing in a type of service, such as temporary or executive recruiting, or type of industry, such as marketing or finance. Focusing your efforts allows you to become an expert in the staffing field for your industry. *Before deciding which niche you might like to make your own, first learn more about the primary categories of staffing services in chapters 2, 3, 4, and 5.*

CASE STUDY: BEING YOUR OWN BOSS

Robin Mee, President
Mee Derby & Company
www.meederby.com
robin@meederby.com

Mee Derby & Company has been a national executive search firm head-quartered in Maryland for 19 years. Mee Derby specializes in placing executives, managers, salespeople, and recruiters in staffing, professional services, and human capital outsourcing.

I always had an entrepreneurial spirit and drive, which is partially what drew my initial interest to the staffing industry. This is an industry in which independent companies can compete in any geographic market. Staffing services can be a local buy, and independent companies can have a national or global reach. My circumstances changed when I found myself laid off due to the impending sale of my employer to a larger company. Forced unemployment threw me into a job search, and while interviewing for jobs, I also researched opening my own firm. After three months of serious consideration, I launched Mee Derby. In part, I wanted to be my own boss, have the ability to drive my income based on my performance, and have the flexibility that comes with running my own company. I wanted Mee Derby to become the most influential search firm in the staffing industry.

Mee Derby is a national search firm that specializes in placing professionals in staffing and workforce management. Ten percent of our work is retained executive search and 90 percent is contingency search for managers, senior sales, and recruiters. We staff the staffing industry.

Words of wisdom for new staffing agency owners:

✓ Do your research.

✓ Invest in technology.

✓ Join the American Staffing Association, attend Staffing World, and join your local ASA chapter.

✓ Subscribe to Staffing Industry Analysts publications.

✓ Focus on a niche.

✓ Hire wisely.

✓ Work in the industry before launching your own company.

✓ Work on your strategic plan every day.

✓ Do not forget this is a sales-driven industry.

✓ Love the work.

✓ Always be honest and ethical.

✓ Stop the buck with you.

2
Administrative Services

An administrative services staffing agency helps find and place administrative employees and secretaries with the its clients. The clients are the companies that hire you to find employees on their behalf. Essentially, you and your business are acting as the liaison and matchmaker between your clients and individuals who are looking for administrative employment.

With this setup, you would be working for the client to find the employees they seek. You would meet with the representative from the business to go over the job for which he or she is seeking candidates and learn what the responsibilities for the job are. Your job is to get to know the company as best as you can so you can identify employees who will fit into the corporate culture and who are qualified to do the job.

While you work to land company clients, also identify qualified administrative professionals to add to your database of candidates. Gathering candidates, even if they are not actively seeking employment, allows you to have their information available if an opportunity arises.

When your client has a position they need to fill, you can use your database of qualified candidates to start scheduling interviews. You also have the option to place online or local classified ads to reach new potential candidates for this specific position. The candidates who respond also become a part of your database, so even if they do not make the cut for this specific job, you are growing your pool of potential candidates for future positions.

Who Are the Clients?

You might have some circumstances in which a large company or corporation uses your services to identify and place an administrative person in the organization. For the most part, however, clients that frequent staffing services for administrative staff are small- to medium-sized businesses. Typical clients fall into the categories of:

- Consultants
- Job seekers
- Businesses with one owner

What is Administrative Work?

The primary type of work associated with administrative services is secretarial. Although some staffing services only place secretaries, administrative staffing agencies broaden the duties employees are expected to perform. Secretaries commonly do more than answer the phone, schedule appointments, and type correspondence. Some of the administrative duties clients might expect employees to perform include the following:

Presentations

Many clients look for administrative staff familiar with using a variety of software and desktop publishing programs. This knowledge primarily is used to put together standard correspondence but can also be used to assemble more complex projects, such as presentations. These can include PowerPoint presentations, handouts, worksheets, and other materials that need to be passed out to the audience.

Other correspondence might include both online and offline invitations; press releases; and brochures, postcards, or other marketing pieces designed with desktop publishing programs for the business owner or manager. Administrative staff might also be responsible for managing contacts in a database for direct mailings or e-mail blasts to customers. These employees can help fulfill almost any administrative task the business owner or manager needs.

Editorial

When a business needs help putting together copy and content for the business, they might seek administrative help with an editorial slant. Editorial help might include writing copy for invitations; press releases; letters; and other marketing, promotional, and communications vehicles that the business uses to interact with its customers. Generally, these employees have extensive experience in composing these materials, and English is their first language. Additional requirements might even be possession of a related degree, such as English or marketing.

Website design

Although an administrative staff member might not exclusively be a website designer, Web design is a task that many small- to medium-sized businesses seek help with in addition to other administrative duties. The business owner or manager might need someone to design and maintain the company website. This includes updating the website with special event information, including dates, times, and addresses. This task might also include updating the website or blog with articles or other information content. For a business that has an online selling component, the employee might need to add new product pictures, descriptions, and shopping cart items to keep the merchandise up-to-date.

Transcription

Transcription is another role an administrative staff professional might be required to fulfill. Companies of all sizes need their meetings and phone conferences recorded and transcribed. Some companies are required to maintain written records of these meetings for legal purposes. Other companies give or sell the transcripts to customers, investors, and others.

Employees

The employees you need to find to fill the positions your clients want are as varied as the duties. First, find candidates who are personable and have the ability to deal with the public. In most cases, the administrative staff is the first contact prospects and customers have with a business. Second, administrative workers also tend to interact with the business's customers on an ongoing basis, which means they have to be customer-service oriented.

The second type of employees you need are those who are able to multitask. Rather than find employees who only have a talent for writing or only have a talent for Web design, find employees who have the ability to do more than one type of work. They need to be familiar with a variety of software programs and tasks. The clients who are looking for administrative staff want qualified people who are able to help them with what they need at a reasonable hourly rate. If they wanted to pay the rates of a professional Web designer, they would go out and hire someone who just does Web design. In these circumstances, your clients need general administrative help at the pay scale and experience level for their needs.

Variety

When opening and running a staffing service that specializes in administrative professionals, be prepared for the variety of work you are asked to do. One client might ask you to find someone who can answer phones and act as the receptionist on a full-time basis. Another client might be looking for a right-hand man or woman who can help him or her with all the daily tasks that come along with running a business.

In addition to job role variances, company variances are also a possibility. You might work with companies that are as small as a one person or as large as multimillion dollar corporations that employ hundreds or thousands of employees at any given time. Their demands are as different as the companies. The demand for employees can vary from year to year or from season to season. Some of these variances depend on the types of companies or industries you choose to work with in providing your staffing services.

Changes in the community can also affect the demand for employees. For example, when automobile companies began a drastic decline in 2008 and 2009, the demand for employees in the Detroit area fell. Unemployment rates rose drastically, and the community went into a major economic decline. Any changes in the business community to which you offer your staffing services will affect your work as a recruiter or staffing provider.

Freedom to Experiment

Starting your staffing service in one direction does not mean that you might not need to take another route or redirect your area of specialty at some point. Test the waters in new markets or industries. Trying out new areas is the best way to determine whether the new direction will offer you success. Your decision to maneuver your business into new areas comes down to assessing the market and your own interests.

The market drives part of the decision to offer new services or work in new industries. It comes back to supply and demand. If you see there an increase in demand for employees in a certain market, industry, or role, you might experiment with reaching out more to the companies and potential employees that fall into this category. In contrast, if you see a decline in a market or industry you already cover, you might want to redirect your current efforts away from this area long enough to test out the new market needs.

Another reason you might choose to operate in a specific staffing niche or industry could relate to your own interests or experience. Many people believe they will be more likely to succeed if they enjoy their work. If you have a special interest in a particular industry or job position or you enjoy working with certain companies, you are much more likely to proactively do what is necessary to be successful in this area of your business. For example, if you enjoy working with creative types, such such as graphic designers, marketing professionals, and copywriters, you might wish to place these types of professionals instead of financial professionals.

Interest does not necessarily require you to have previous experience or knowledge with the area. If you have a genuine interest in a market or industry, you tend to have a thirst to research, learn, and acquire the knowledge you need to work your staffing services magic for that area. If you have a burning desire to recruit for and staff the pharmaceutical industry, you can research the top companies in the market, learn about the various employment positions involved in running pharmaceutical companies, and pull research reports on the industry as a whole. Take the time to research the positions and learn more about the companies in your area of interest. Even if you focused on the financial industry, it is possible to fulfill your interests by making the switch to the creative industry.

3

The "Temp" Agency and Contractors

The temp agency places temporary workers with its company clients. A temporary employee might work for a company for one day or have a contract to work with the company for the next six months. The employee will work on a short-term basis of less than one year. Companies will use short-term workers to fill in for absent employees or add to existing staff during busy times. Many staffing services find employees who will work on a temp-to-perm basis for companies. In a temp-to-perm situation, a client pays you an additional fee for employees you placed who take a permanent position with the company. In a temp-to-perm situation, the services you provide allow the companies to try out an employee before deciding to hire them on a full-time, permanent basis.

Temporary staffing services make up the bulk of the staffing service industry. When you are running a temp agency, you have to focus your work in two areas. Businesses, companies, and organizations will turn to you to find temporary workers for them, but you will also need a pool of temporary workers you can pull from when the need arises. In some situations, you might not have an individual who fits the current needs of a client, so you might have to recruit temporary workers from outside your pool. You will have some temp workers who only have an interest in working one or two days here and there, and you will have others who do not mind signing on as a contractor for the company for months at a time.

The Client

The lines of distinction for the types of companies that work with temp agencies are blurred. Your company clients will range from one-person businesses to small- and medium-sized businesses to large corporations. A small business with five employees is just as likely to have a need for temporary help as a large corporation is to need someone to fill in for an employee while he or she is on an extended vacation or leave of absence.

Generalize or Find a Niche Market?

You can go one of two ways when you decide to open and operate a temp or contract agency. First, you can choose to offer general temp services. You agree to find an endless type of workers for the businesses that are your clients, which includes everything from a secretary to an engineer to a mailroom clerk. The advantage of supplying general types of temporary workers is it does not limit your ability to help a client. Whether the company has a need for a receptionist or a scientist, you can help them when you offer general staffing services.

The second option for opening a temp or contract staffing agency is to specialize in a particular industry or niche, which also has its advantages.

First, it allows you to narrow your client search to certain types of companies. Second, it allows you to narrow your pool of workers you keep in your database and send out on jobs. Specialization also provides the opportunity to become an expert in the industry, field, or market that you serve. If you decide to specialize in creative professionals, such as graphic designers and marketing writers, all the companies with a need for these types of workers will know you are the go-to staffing agency.

Your decision to generalize or specialize your staffing services should not be rash. Instead, base your decision on market research, your experience, the economic situation of the market or industry you are considering, and what your competition is doing.

Market research boils down to the supply and demand in the market you wish to serve. Supply and demand in the staffing industry has two aspects: your client companies and a supply of temporary employees to fill the needs of the companies. If you live in a manufacturing town, you might want to focus your efforts on placing industrial workers. Almost any business has a need for administrative or office staff workers. If your focus remains on office positions, you can still narrow your niche within this type of work. For example, focus on high-end administrative staff, such as personal and executive assistants, rather than receptionists and file clerks.

You should also consider your own work experience and knowledge before deciding on a niche or specialty. When you have experience working in a specific field, this gives you an advantage over a staffing service owner who does not know the behind-the-scenes information that you do. You will also be better able to discuss the position and find employees who fit the criteria for the work. If you have legal experience, you might decide to focus your efforts on placing legal workers in law firms and other legal agencies.

Having experience and knowledge does not make it natural for you to specialize. A major factor in your decision should also be a financial assessment. You need to figure out whether your business can make money in the area of expertise you are considering. Although your love for a particular industry or niche might fuel your drive, all your hard work will be wasted if you cannot find company clients or workers to fill the positions. You might have a medical background and decide you want to focus on medical employees. The problem is it can be difficult to land hospitals and medical facilities as clients. Without these types of organizations as your clients, making money will be difficult because you will not have any clients paying your fees.

The final assessment should be competitive research. Never underestimate the value of knowing your competition. Make a list of the other staffing services in your market. Which ones target the same types of companies and workers you will? Find out which services they are offering and how much they are charging for their services. Take a detailed look at your competition when you narrow down your choices. The best way to find information about your competition might be to visit their establishments. Be creative about how you obtain the information you need.

Some sources of information on competition include:

- Yellow Pages: This directory provides you with the telephone number and location of your competitors.

- Chambers of commerce: These organizations have lists of local businesses. Verify whether the list is comprehensive or just contains chamber members.

- Local newspapers: Study the local advertisements and help wanted ads.

- American Staffing Association: This organization provides information, news, education, and more on the staffing industry. Find it online at **www.americanstaffing.net**.

Evaluating the competition

The staffing services business is highly competitive. How can you keep up with the constant flow of information detailing which companies are doing what, where they are doing it, how well they do it, and what they charge?

Attending local professional group events will help this process. Whether you visit your area's chamber of commerce or the local chapter of the American Staffing Association, your associates and peers will likely bring bits of information you can use to understand the competitive atmosphere that surrounds you. You can invite responses from former clients or suppliers by simply asking for information.

One rule that most business people accept is to not speak negatively about your competitors in public. If you bad-mouth a competitor, the client often will feel less comfortable with you even if you are more experienced and qualified than the person you are putting down. Staying polite and professional by emphasizing what you do best and basically ignoring what the competition does is socially acceptable and likely to bring you more business.

Creating a formula that includes overhead and profit requirements for your business is vital before beginning to quote prices to potential clients. It might not be a good idea to find out what your competition charges and duplicate that rate without checking whether it works for you. Perhaps your competition is losing money, or it might have priced its services too high. Competitors have different cost structures. Shape your bids on the cost structure of your business, including your overhead, your employees if applicable, and your profit goals. Although knowing what your competitors charge for the services you plan to offer or are already providing is important, your basic pricing method has to be localized to be effective.

National average prices for services are of limited use to a business startup though a look at trends for the past several years might be helpful to determining whether the work is likely to increase. The U.S. Department of Labor tracks information about a number of workforce and industry segments in its *Occupational Outlook Handbook* on the Department of Labor website at **www.dol.gov**.

CASE STUDY: NICHE
TO BE RICH

Cari Kraft, Owner
Jacobs Management Group Inc.
1420 Walnut Street, Suite 1100
Philadelphia, PA 19102
(215) 732-6400
www.jacobsmgt.com

Jacobs Management Group Inc., with Cari Kraft at the helm, specializes in executive placement in the pharmaceutical, medical device, biotechnology, and technology industries. When Kraft first began with the firm, she was an employee, but she was set on buying the company at some point in the future, which she did.

Kraft opts to run the business from a corporate office. Because the positions they place tend to be at an executive level, having a corporate setting helps to create the professional image of the firm in the minds of both its clients and candidates. Another advantage of running the business from a corporate office location is it provides a location for the team to meet in one place and support each other. Kraft says the downtown Philadelphia location has also given them the ability to pull employees from a number of locations. The costs of operating and maintaining the downtown office and limitations in the lease timing for expansion are two of the disadvantages.

Kraft says establishing a niche is one of the primary pieces of advice she would offer to someone starting a staffing business. Establishing a niche paints the business as the expert that everyone needs to find employees in the area. A niche also allows the owner and eventually the employees of the staffing service to focus their efforts and refine their skills in placement services in the specialty.

It also creates a situation in which the staffing firm can build a pool of highly qualified candidates and contacts. Whether the candidates are in the market for a new position, they know other people in their specialty and can refer the staffing professional to someone who might be interested in the job. Clients also come to recognize the firm for its large number of contacts, which also attracts new clients and keeps existing clients for the long haul.

Setting Fees

When it comes to setting the fees for placing temporary workers, the markup can vary greatly according to the type of position and the region of the country. A temporary agency in Los Angeles makes 25 to 75 percent of the wages of the temporary employee depending on the type of position, the region, and the industry. The fee you charge can also vary by the industry. An Oregon staffing agency that specializes in placing temporary staff in law firms and legal entities makes 70 percent of the employee's wages.

You can charge anywhere from 20 to 75 percent on top of the wages of the employees you are placing with the company as your fee. Some of the factors you should consider when setting your fees include:

- Competition
- Client relationship
- Industry or niche

Your fees do not have to be etched in stone. For example, if you charge a minimum of 25 percent but have an opportunity to land a new client you want, you might be willing to lower your fee to 20 percent because that is what it was paying its previous staffing agency. As situations change, your fees might change. If the market has a shortage of available employees but you have a pool of coveted professionals, you could charge a premium to place them with the client companies on a temporary basis.

The pay rate is the fee or rate the staffing service pays the employee. Temporary agencies, which employ the workers at a client's location, pay these fees.

Finding Employees

When you are running a temp agency or any type of staffing agency, you have a few concerns regarding employees. The first area you need to tackle is hiring the employees you need to run your own office. When you first start out in the temporary staffing business, you might operate the business on your own. Although you can open your agency and even operate it for some time completely on your own, your need for help managing all the different aspects of the business will grow as the demand for your services grows.

Internal employees

Some of the permanent employees you will need in your office include:

- An administrative assistant: The administrative assistant will be your right hand. The assistant might also back up the other management positions in the office by answering phones, taking messages, managing files, and completing other administrative tasks.

- Bookkeeper/payroll: The bookkeeper or payroll assistant handles the payroll for your office and for the temporary workers you supply to the client companies. The bookkeeper also acts as the liaison between your business and its clients for billing, collecting payments, and managing collections for past due accounts.

- Office manager: The office manager is responsible for overseeing the office operations on a daily basis. This might be your role when you start, but you will need to free up your time to land new clients as your business grows.

- Permanent placement administrator: This administrator handles all the aspects of running the temp-to-perm placements. He or she recruits, interviews, and selects candidates for temp-to-perm positions. He or she also works with the clients and the employees through the placement process.

If you happen to place a large pool of temporary employees with one client company, you might also need to hire an on-site administrator. This administrator oversees and manages the temporary employees who are working at the single location. A human resources manager or equivalent on site will give the large pool of temp or contract workers in one location a representative they can turn to for payroll, health benefits, and other needs not related to the physical work they are performing for the client company.

Other optional positions include a sales associate, recruiter, and a receptionist. As the staffing business grows, you have a need to delegate more responsibilities away from yourself. You also might want to segregate the responsibilities of each employee so they truly become an expert and specialist in their position.

- Sales associate: This employee helps you land new client accounts. In addition, they often manage customer service issues with existing clients. Sales associates are out of the office more than they are in the office because they are out in the field trying to sign on new company accounts.

- Recruiter: The recruiter is responsible for identifying candidates who fit the individual job orders your agency has for its clients. The recruiter is also responsible for managing the database or pool of candidates by putting résumés and contact information for candidates into the database for possible opportunities in the future.

- Receptionist: You will find that the busier your business gets, the more the phone will ring. Your business will receive calls from the companies and the temporary workers and candidates for positions. Although your administrative assistant might be able to handle the influx of calls at first, there might come a time when he or she is simply too busy to answer the phone and manage all the other administrative tasks. When this occurs, it might be time to separate the phone duties from the administrative assistant and hire a full-time receptionist.

Temporary workers

Even though recruiting employees for your own office can be a challenge, one of the biggest challenges of running a temp or contract agency is recruiting the temporary workers and temp-to-perm workers you need for your business-client relationships to function and be lucrative. Some people want a full-time job they know has the potential to last for years. Other people are content with looking for positions they know have an end date.

Identifying and recruiting temporary workers might be especially challenging because these are special types of individuals. Temporary workers range from stay-at-home moms looking for extra money to college students looking to generate income in between attending classes and studying. You might also have pools of candidates who are professionals in their field but are currently unemployed for one reason or another. The skill levels, experiences, and statuses of temporary workers can range greatly.

The keys to finding and employing temporary workers are fishing for candidates in the right places and establishing a proper screening process. The three primary ways to locate temp workers include advertising, running special promotions, and going after recent college graduates.

Advertisements

Advertisements for your business will have two main focuses: general business promotion and the job positions you are trying to fill for your clients. In addition to the types of advertisements you run, you also have choices when it comes to the media you use to run your advertisements. You can choose from television, newspapers, specialty or trade publications, business cards, the yellow pages, radio, the Internet, fliers, brochures, and newsletters.

General advertisements about your business expose your business and your service offering to both potential clients and temporary workers. You might run a display ad in your local newspaper with the name of your business and a headline stating, "Hiring Daily!" Under the headline, offer bullet points on the benefits you offer temporary workers, such as vacation pay and health insurance. You might also wish to list that you have both full- and part-time assignments available for temporary workers. Include the contact information for your business.

An advertisement for specific types of workers can follow the same format. The headline might say, "Hiring Now!" The bullet points would speak specifically about the position you are trying to fill and the benefits workers will receive as a temporary employee for your staffing service.

- Newspapers: Local newspapers are your best bet for attracting local candidates. Newspaper advertisements tend to best attract general candidates or candidates for a specific position. If you are looking for candidates at the professional level, administrative workers, and industrial workers, major newspapers tend to pull in more and better candidates. In the Miami area, the major newspaper is the *Miami Herald*, but in the Fort Lauderdale area, it is *The Sun-Sentinel*.

- Specialty or trade publications: When you are targeting specific types of workers, consider specialty papers or trade publications. Specialty papers might include neighborhood papers or religious or business publications. Trade publications target individuals who work in a particular sector or industry.

- Business cards: One of the primary sources of advertising for a temp or contract agency is the business card, which is an essential component of marketing your business when you are networking or when you strike up a conversation with someone who is a prospective temporary worker or client. You want your card to portray that you offer short-term and temporary work options rather than full-time and permanent positions. Your card should have your name, title, contact information, and the logo of your company on the front. You can place business cards on community bulletin boards; hand them out at local events; or give them to friends, acquaintances, and anyone you meet who is a potential worker or client.

Also, be sure to maximize the space you have on your business cards, which means using both the front and the back of the card. The front of the card can contain all the contact information for the business, and the back of the card can provide additional information. Specify the types of employment opportunities you offer, which include temporary and temp-to-perm work. The back of your business card should also address the benefits the workers will have access to when working for your agency, such as health insurance, flexible hours, and top wages. Provide enough information on your business card so it acts as a stand-alone seller for your business. This means someone who finds your card on the street or on a bulletin board can quickly understand what your business does and how it benefits him or her to contact you.

You have a variety of ways you can design and print business cards for your staffing service. The most expensive way to obtain business cards is to hire a graphic designer to design the cards and then send the file off to a printer to have the cards printed. Websites such as Vistaprint (**www.vistaprint.com**) and 48hourprint.com (**www.48hourprint.com**) have professionally designed business card templates you can customize, personalize, and print at a reduced rate. You also have the option to upload your own design, so even if you have a graphic designer create the card, you can print your card through one of these companies for less than most local printers will charge.

Desktop publishing programs also make business card templates available for you to create business cards. You can print these cards on your own printer using business card stock available at any major office supply or stationary store. Although this might be the least expensive way to get the business cards you need, it does require a time investment. Another disadvantage to creating and printing your own business cards is it might cheapen the image of your company.

- Yellow pages: When you operate in a specific geographic area, it is wise to place an ad in the yellow pages of the local phone book. For these purposes, run a general ad about your business. As a temporary staffing service, this should include the name of your business and the types of services you provide. The ad is listed under employment or staffing. Write the ad so it speaks to both potential workers and the companies that might hire you for their staffing needs.

- Radio: Running radio ads, also known as spots, is another effective way to get the word out in your local area. This form of advertising can be a bit pricey depending on the time of day and the number of ads you run. When you start out, you might not be able to afford this form of advertising, but as your company and your marketing budget grow, radio advertising might come into play.

- Internet: Running job advertisements, both free and paid, is a highly effective way to reach potential candidates for temp positions. Free classified ad sites such as Craigslist (**www.craigslist.org**), eBay Classifieds (**www.ebayclassifieds.com**), BackPage (**www.backpage.com**), and Indeed (**www.indeed.com**) are all options. Each site allows you to choose a specific location and fill in the details of the position you are trying to fill. You can also run general ads on each of these sites in an attempt to build up your database of clients and candidates.

- Fliers: Printing up fliers allows you take advantage of basic marketing. Post the fliers on bulletin boards at local hot spots, such as the grocery store, library, and coffee houses. Some businesses might allow you to leave a stack of fliers for their customers. You should even be able to leave a stack of fliers at the local unemployment office. Other options include churches, community centers, the local chamber of commerce, colleges, civic organizations or club offices, Welcome Wagon agencies, and real estate offices. Welcome Wagon agencies are companies that assemble information for residents who have recently relocated to the area. A representative visits the home of the new resident and provides an information package that includes contact information, coupons, and general information about local services and businesses.

- Brochures: Use brochures as marketing tools at trade shows, career expos, and client meetings. A business card provides a limited amount of space in which to explain the service you offer and what you can do for business clients and candidates, but a brochure provides you with additional space in which to sell the reader on working with your staffing service.

- Newsletters: As you start to build a contact database, you can also use a company newsletter to communicate with business clients and candidates. In addition to providing useful and informational content, you can also include specific job listings.

Special promotions

In addition to some of the general marketing tactics you can use, you also have the option of running special promotions and campaigns. One type of special promotion is to set up a table at a job or career fair taking place in your local community. Career fairs tend to attract all sorts of candidates and even allow you to mix and mingle with businesses in the area that are trying to attract qualified candidates.

You can even host your own job fair. You can do this at your own office or location or rent a space at a local hotel. Hosting your own job fair requires you and your staff to do a large amount of work to promote and market the job fair. When you participate in a job fair another organization hosts, you should find out how the organizers plan to promote the event, but you are also responsible for promoting the event on your own. Send out e-mails and distribute fliers and use other avenues available to you to promote your attendance at the event.

Rather than refer to your job fair as a job fair, you can instead refer to it as an open house. When you host an open house of your staffing business, you might even be able to get it on the community calendar of your local newspapers, television stations, and radio stations. Getting the open house on the community calendars is a complimentary form of advertising for your business and your event.

College graduates

One large pool of temporary candidates is graduates from community colleges and universities in your area. When you leave fliers at these educational facilities, especially in the career center, you have the opportunity to reach both students who need to work while attending school and recent college graduates who need full-time employment. You can promote your staffing service in these institutions in a couple different ways. Start by contacting the career center of each institution to find out which services and programs the school offers for staffing services and companies.

Many of these schools host their own job fairs on a regular basis. Attending these events exposes your staffing service to current and graduating students. It even exposes your service to the alumni of the school. Schools also allow job postings on the school's website and in campus publications, such as the school newspaper, special career publications, and career fair agendas for free or a small cost.

Temp-to-perm workers

Before you start attracting temp-to-perm candidates, you should have a process in place for how to assess each application and résumé you receive. Also consider the different ways in which candidates will contact your office: walk-in, appointment, phone call, e-mail, online application submission, and community meetings and events.

Three of the primary pieces of information to collect from possible candidates include employment and personal references, employment records, and skills tests. You should start by creating a form you can either fill out with candidates as you talk or have the candidate fill out him or herself. It can be an employment application, which you can create in a word processing program or download in template form from the Internet. *You can find a sample candidate reference form on the CD-ROM.* Be sure the application collects all the personal and professional information you need from a candidate up front. Also, create a hard copy and electronic version so you can send it to the candidate to complete or hand it to them when you meet in person.

Go through the information after you collect it. Verify you have all the information you need and you have copies of the candidates' résumés accompanying the forms. Enter the information or scan it into your database program.

After collecting the data and paperwork you need, the next logical step is to schedule an interview with the candidates you have selected. If you receive a blind résumé or application or one that does not fit a current need you have, you do not have to schedule an interview with the candidate until an opportunity arises. When you are interested in a candidate on paper is the time to conduct a face to face meeting so you can put a face to the name, ask questions, and uncover additional information you might not have been able to glean from his or her paperwork.

The tests you give to candidates are up to you. Some of the tests you should consider include:

- Drug tests
- Typing tests

- Computer skills tests
- Terms or knowledge tests for specific industries

When you are running a temp agency, you are working to both attract clients that need employees and also candidates to fill the positions your clients have. Your clients are the businesses, companies, and organizations that turn to you to find temporary workers for them. As a temp agency, you also have to have a pool of temporary workers that you can pull from when needs for each of your clients arise. In some situations, you might not have an individual who fits the needs of a client, so you might have to recruit temporary workers from outside your pool who do fit the needs.

When you have a situation in which a temporary worker turns into a permanent worker for a client company, you can charge the client company a conversion fee or rate.

Working through the steps provided to you in this chapter will build the foundation for each side of your staffing service — the client and the candidate side.

4

The Executive Recruiter

The simple explanation of what an executive recruiter does is contract with a company to find a suitable candidate for a specific position the company needs to fill. The daily tasks involved in the process are, however, a bit more complex. So what does a day in the life of an executive recruiter look like?

The truth is cold calling prospective clients, especially when you first launch your business, takes up the majority of your day. Many companies that hire at an executive level have their own internal staffing employees and human resources workers who are looking for employees. They might not think to contact an executive recruiter or only turn to an executive recruiter when they have exhausted all other measures. You want these companies to know you exist and know your areas of specialty are when and if they need you. Timing is everything, and there are times when they will need you right when you call. After all, if you do not have a client, you do not have a position to try to fill, which also means you are not getting paid. Even when you have one or more clients you are working with to fill positions, you should still devote time on daily basis to cold calling and searching for new clients. Many successful recruiters believe recruiting is a people business and a numbers game.

Recruiting is a people business because you have to talk to people. You have to know whom to talk to, where to find the people to talk to, and what to say once you get the opportunity to talk to them. It is a numbers game because you must talk to many people to succeed in this business. The more people you talk to and the more effective your talks are, the better you will succeed in executive recruiting.

Paying attention to details, having the ability to negotiate deals, listening and observing well, and having patience are all qualities a successful recruiter must possess. Beyond possessing these personal and professional traits, successful recruiters also follow a proven formula that seems to take them down the path of success faster and more often than other processes.

#1: Land the client: You have to land the company or client first. You land a client through your marketing efforts, including cold calling, because they have a specific position they are looking to fill. You might also need to evaluate the urgency or the need for filling the position. Obviously, a more urgent need to fill the position is better for you because it means the client is motivated. You should complete a candidate profile with the client to get an idea of who their ideal candidate is so you can go into your database and out into the world to find that person. Finally, work out the fee agreement and get the client to sign it before you move forward. Whether you are working on a retainer or contingency basis, put everything in writing and have the client sign and agree to the terms and conditions in the agreement. *You can learn more about the difference between working on a retainer or contingency basis on page 63.*

#2: Speak to the hiring manager: You often speak to the human resources manager or owner of a company to land the client and the **job**

order, which is the order from the client that he or she wants you to work on filling the position. If you are not speaking to the person who will be directly supervising the employee you are seeking, you should. Go through a needs analysis with the hiring manager to get a complete picture of the candidate who should be working in this position. Discuss the role the manager is trying to fill and the specific personality traits, experience, and skills the hiring manager is looking for in a new employee. Gather the technical duties and responsibilities of the position and talk with the manager about the traits and characteristics of the previous three people who successfully worked in the position. Find out why they were successful. Also ask why the person who filled the previous position is no longer with the company. These are major clues to finding the next successful candidate. If the company is creating a new position, they still have in mind the responsibilities and characteristics of the person they want to hire. You should also be able to help the company identify what they might be looking for in an employee based on the job role the person will fill.

#3: Make a plan: After you have gathered all the clues and information you need, it is now time to make a plan on how you are going identify and reel in the best candidates for the position. Determine all the places you need to go to find candidates. Write out a description of the position you will offer to candidates that presents the job in the best possible light. This should include the top three to five selling points on both the company performing the hiring and the position itself. Match the successful traits of the position and the places you can find people who have these traits.

#4: Compile your research: These steps all come before you ever pick up the phone to find candidates. The proper planning and preparation up front tends to provide you with the guide or road map you need to identify the top possible candidates for the job. Start by making a list of all the sources and resources you have or can get to find candidates. You should also include companies on the list at which you can go fishing for employees. Think, too, about job titles that are different from the job title you are looking to fill but performs the same or a similar role. Many executive recruiters submit the list of possible companies to the client so the client can approve or remove companies on the list. Clients might not want a recruiter to visit certain companies to find potential employees for various reasons. A difference in the caliber of employees, training methods, and business practices are three of the reasons a client might not want you to visit a particular business. Other companies might have brought employees over from said company before and had poor experiences. The hiring company might have had previous employees move over to a competitor and do not want to risk attracting these former employees back to the organization.

#5: Start the search: After completing the first four steps, you are finally ready to start searching for the possible candidates for the position. Once you pull résumés from your database or use your other resources to identify possible candidates, you have to filter out the candidates who do not fit the job requirements and prioritize the remaining candidates. Start with the best possible candidate and further qualify him or her with an initial phone interview. Complete phone interviews for any of the remaining candidates, and then narrow down the options further to schedule face to face interviews. After conducting your interviews, compile your list of final candidates. Prioritize these again so the best candidate is at the top of your list but still have backup candidates in case the client does not like the candidate or the candidate does not like the client. Also, if the candidate starts working for the company but quits or gets fired during the probationary period, you can then turn to the other candidates on your list as options.

#6: References and background information check: From the list of finalists, take the time to check references and background. Some clients have specific checks they want you to make, but you should check both personal references and employment references. You also need to verify any credentials the candidate claims and review the candidate résumés for any changes or modifications that need to be made before going any further in the process.

#7:Candidate preparation: The final candidates are the ones you want to interview with the client. Before sending the candidates, you also want to spend time preparing the candidate for the interview. Establish the expectations for the job and explain the company culture and the people they will be interviewing with at the company. The more prepared the candidate is before the interview, the better his or her chances are of impressing the company representatives responsible for hiring them.

#8: Client preparation: On the flip side, you also need to take the time to prepare the client. Go over with the hiring supervisor how the candidate fulfills each of the points the company is looking for. Highlight the top points about the candidate, such as experience, education, and awards. You should also discuss the career goals of the candidate and the interview process the candidate went through with your business before the interview with the company.

#9: Postmortem on the interview: Right after the interview, you want to speak with both the candidate and the client. Get a feel from the candidate how the interview went and whether the candidate is interested in the position. Then do the same with the client. When you talk to the client, they might be ready to make an offer to the candidate, at which point the negotiation process begins.

#10: Offer acceptance: Once the offer is presented to the candidate and he or she accepts it, your work is not over. Finalize any remaining details such as start date and get everything in writing.

#11: Follow-up: Stay in touch with both the candidate and the employer up until and after the candidate starts. Confirm all the details leading up to the start date, talk with both on the start date, and then schedule regular check-in calls for the months following the start date.

The Client

The clients that hire executive recruiters are often major corporations. This does not mean, however, that smaller and mid-sized companies do not use the services of executive recruiting firms as well. The types or size of the companies that use your services directly relates to your area of specialty. For example, if you specialize in finding pharmaceutical employees, pharmaceutical companies are likely to be your clients. If you specialize in marketing professionals, however, your clients range from small, privately owned businesses to large multinational corporations with offices spread out around the globe.

Ultimately, you are working for the client that pays you, but you are also a liaison between the client and the candidates. Although the candidates are not paying your fee, until you place the right candidate in the position, you are not getting paid either.

Contacts

Executive recruiters tend to specialize in a specific industry or types of positions rather than act as general recruiters. You can find recruiters who specialize in law enforcement, finance, marketing, electrical engineering, and almost any other industry you come across. Some recruiters specialize in two areas, such as sales professionals for the flower industry or marketing professionals in the finance industry.

The primary reason that executive recruiters tend to specialize is two-fold. First, it allows the recruiter to gather knowledge and use experience in one area. Executive recruiters advance more in their career by becoming a master of one specialty instead of trying to accommodate everyone. The second reason executive recruiters specialize is it allows the recruiter to build contacts in a specific industry. This is vital to the success of an executive recruiting business. You will need to call on these contacts for a myriad of reasons. One reason is you want to be able to land these types of companies as clients. Also, you want to be able to call on the employees of these companies because they likely know others in the same profession who might be looking for a new job when you have a position to fill. Finally, when these employees are looking to move on in the industry, you want them to think of you as the expert in the industry who can move them to the next level in their career.

For you, specializing in one field or industry immensely simplifies your role. You can truly focus your efforts in all aspects of your business. You can use any experience you have in the industry and apply it to finding clients and finding candidates to fill positions. You can easily and quickly build up your database of contacts on both the client and candidate side. Finally, it positions you as the credible expert that employers and employees in the industry need to work with when hiring or looking for work.

Contingency or Retainer?

Executive recruiters generally work on a contract, which is either a contingency contract or a retainer. How you decide to work as an executive recruiter is up to you. Some recruiters work either way depending on the client.

When you work on contingency, you are working on spec. This means a client has a specific position they want you to work on filling for them. The hitch is the client will not pay you until you fill the position. The other hitch to working on a contingency basis is you tend to be working in competition with other recruiters. In other words, you do not have exclusivity in finding a candidate for the client, so it is highly likely you and half a dozen other executive recruiters are all working to fill the same position at the same time. This also means you might end up spending hours and hours working on filling the position but never reap any monetary benefits for doing so.

When you work on a retainer, however, the client pays you up front to work on finding a candidate to fill the position. When you work on a retainer, you also need a guarantee in the contract you have with the client. The first guarantee is you will work until you find a qualified candidate to fill the position. The second guarantee tends to be if the candidate the client hires leaves within a certain period, such as the first 90 days, you will work to find another candidate without earning any additional money. Retainer work is exclusively yours, so you are not in direct competition with other executive recruiters to fill the same position. The contingency option is the one two-thirds to three-quarters of recruiters use. The rest working on retainer or a combination of retainer and contingency.

Recruiters who are new to the industry tend to work on a contingency basis while more experienced recruiters working on executive level management positions tend to work on a retainer. Recruiters who work on a contingency basis also tend to work on 30 to 40 positions at a time, but retained recruiters tend to focus their efforts on filling only a few positions at a time.

Beyond the pros and cons to you as the recruiter, there are pros and cons for each type of work to the clients as well. To a client, a recruiter working on a retainer has more of an incentive to find the ideal candidate for the position than when they are working on a contingency basis. Because a retainer pays the recruiter up front, clients tend to feel you will work harder to find the most appropriate person for the job. In addition, you have more time to track down the right candidate because you are working on filling fewer positions than if you were working on a contingency basis.

Other companies prefer to work with recruiters on a contingency basis. One reason is the human resources department might be doing its own recruiting while you are recruiting for the position. If the company finds an ideal candidate before you do, they are not obliged to pay you. Also, working on contingency allows the company to work with several recruiters at a time, which increases the number of possible candidates presented to the company.

CASE STUDY: SETTING FEES IS NOT SET IN STONE

Deidre Siegel, Owner
PEAR Core Solutions Inc.
135 Crossways Park Drive, Suite 403
Woodbury, NY 11797
(516) 496-PEAR (7327), ext. 301
www.pearcoresolutions.com

Deidre Siegel opened PEAR Core Solutions Inc. after years of using the services of other staffing agencies and executive recruiters for the hiring needs of the company she was working for during those times. Siegel simply felt there was a better way to serve the employer and the job seeker. Having always had an owner mentality, she felt confident her vision was a viable one, so she decided to branch out on her own in 2003. Her idea was to implement a flat rate fee structure in addition to the percentage of the annual salary.

To test the waters, Siegel started PEAR Core Solutions Inc. solution out of a home office. Growth of the business and the need to add employees to the staff led to running the business from a commercial office space. PEAR Core Solutions Inc. is an executive placement firm, so it adds to the professional image of the business to have a professional office space.

When it comes to setting and charging fees for clients, Siegel says she chooses from one of two options. She either charges the client a flat fee or a percentage of the first year's annual salary of the employee that has been placed. She chose these fee structures for two different reasons:

The percentage of the annual salary is a fee structure that is commonly known and used in the staffing industry. The flat fee was Siegel's idea to provide a different type of structure to clients. After more than eight years in business, Siegel's idea is a viable one, but she admits it does not work for every client, which is why she provides the percentage option. The flat rate fee structure does provide some clients with a cap on how much money they have to come up with out of their budget to cover the hiring of the position they need to fill.

High Research, High Rewards

Finding the best candidates for an open position requires a thorough knowledge of the field, the ability to find candidates, and the persuasiveness to bring the candidate and client together for a mutually beneficial outcome. The better you are at putting your knowledge, experience, and research skills to work, the more likely you are to identify the most ideal candidate for the position. Your reward for being this matchmaker is your fee, which can be anywhere from 25 to 30 percent of the candidate's first year of pay plus benefits.

Treadmill — No Way to Stop

Running an executive recruiting staffing service does not end when you land your first client or even when you are juggling multiple clients. The one-person operation, or even a recruiting agency with three to four employees, ends up running with the treadmill effect. The treadmill effect refers to the fact it is difficult to get off the treadmill while it is still running. A recruiting business rests on the knowledge and expertise of the owner, who might be the only true asset the company has. This means if the owner retires, the business ends with him or her. If a recruiter who specializes in a particular area leaves a multi-recruiter firm, the area of specialty might walk out of the door with the recruiter until the firm finds someone with the contacts, experience, knowledge, and expertise in the same industry to fill the spot.

5

Planning Ahead

No matter which type of staffing service you decide to open, successful businesses share common characteristics. Although these characteristics can apply to any business, these especially apply to a staffing service business. The six essential factors a successful staffing service business possesses include:

1. **Passion:** Staffing service business owners who love matching employees with employers, working with people, and making a difference in people's lives tend to successfully start and run a staffing service. When you possess a passion for your work and your business, it becomes more than a business to you; it becomes a way of life.

2. **A strategic plan:** When you have a strategic plan in writing that outlines where your staffing service is today, where you want it to be tomorrow, and what you need to do to take it there, you have a solid business foundation on which to build.

3. **Excellent customer relations:** Customers in any business are the key component to success because without customers paying you, your business will not get off the ground financially. A staffing service is a people business and makes customer service the hallmark of success.

4. **Quality, reliability, and service emphasis:** You want your clients to believe you provide quality candidates, and you want candidates to believe you offer employment opportunities with high-quality employers. You want both sides to be able to rely on you for their employee and employment needs. Finally, the level of service you provide should be stellar because it is what keeps your clients coming back to you for more high-quality candidates to fill their positions.

5. **Regular evaluation:** The owner should regularly evaluate and monitor procedures, services, pricing, and all the strategic necessities of the business. You might find the candidates for your temp service need résumé services because you are constantly counseling and advising them on how to update and revise their résumés. If this is the case, consider adding résumé services to your service menu.

6. **Flexibility:** A flexible business remains successful as it adapts readily to changes in the industry, technology, and market.

Almost everyone has dreamed of owning his or her own business. Often, these dreams are the result of dealing with difficult bosses, low pay, long hours, swing shifts, and other frustrations that come from working for someone else. In the safe confines of the imagination, the vision of owning a business is immensely satisfying: You are your own boss, you make your own decisions, and you do not have to answer to anyone else. What could be better?

Although there are elements of truth in this vision of business ownership, it is also true that in reality, business owners have problems, too. The problems are different from the frustrations employees face, but they are just as serious. You will want to know your personal capacity for dealing with the problems of business ownership before you jump out of the workforce and take over the boss's chair.

CASE STUDY: CASH FLOW PLANS ARE NOT OPTIONAL

Michael Pope, Owner
Captain Recruiter
1450 Sutter St #537
San Francisco, CA 94109
(415) 264-5223
www.captainrecruiter.com

Michael Pope always wanted to provide a more personalized and less sterile recruiting service at an affordable price. He started off working at a staffing agency that catered to large companies, such as Walmart, HP, and Apple, and smaller companies that are not well-known. Pope's experience recruiting for larger companies felt impersonal and mechanical to him even though it was lucrative. He found the work more fun and interesting when it was for small businesses.

After about a year of working for another person's staffing agency, he found himself wanting to do things his own way. Money was never the driving factor for Pope, and it was hard for him to test the possibility of going out on his own while working full-time for sometime else, so after 14 months on the job, he gave his notice and started his own firm, Captain Recruiting.

The timing, however, might not have been ideal. Pope feels he went out on his own too early. Although he does not know if it would have been any different had he waited, he does know it took him almost 18 months to start making any real money from the business. Pope admits it was almost four years before he felt as though he knew what he was doing. After being an employee all his life before starting his own firm, he was unprepared to run a business at the beginning.

He did not have any savings or any clients. The only recruiting experience he had at the time was based on a model that he despised, which is what propelled him to start his own firm and do it his own way. Pope says it did teach him some valuable lessons he would like to pass on to anyone considering starting a staffing firm.

First, a cash cushion is a necessity, not an option. Next, staffing firms have two channels of business, from clients and even from job candidates. This means staffing professionals need to treat both sides of the equation with care, professionalism, and kindness. Start a blog, and fill it with valuable content on the staffing industry, the staffing firm, and information clients and candidates will find relevant and useful.

Make all your invoices state "due upon receipt" because it will always take 30 days longer to get paid than the deadline indicates. Pick a niche and specialize, but specialize in a specific position rather than a specific skill. Learn to sell because otherwise you have to depend on referrals and luck to land a new customer on your own. Find someone who can reliably do administrative work, such as scheduling interviews and entering data. Give this person clear direction and develop out a system for getting the work done.

Pope learned all these lessons, some of them the hard way, which led to the successful operation of his business. He admits, however, the obstacles he had to overcome might not have existed if he had timed the opening of his business and gained the right experience better.

The Necessary Research

Because a recruiter or staffing service might specialize in an industry rather than a local area, you also have the potential to offer your services across the country. If this is the case, you will need to conduct some national research as well. A 2009 issue of *Forbes* magazine listed the ten best metro and small metro areas in which to start a business. Criteria for the ratings included local cost of doing business, crime rate, educational attainment, living costs, projected income, and job growth. You might want to also add some local market research on per capita income levels, housing prices, family sizes, and other factors likely to impact business. Two of the areas in the list were in South Dakota and two were in Indiana.

Best Small-Metro Cities to Work — Best Areas for Business and Careers:

- Sioux Falls, South Dakota (#3 in cost of doing business)
- Greenville, North Carolina (#4 in cost of doing business)
- Morgantown, West Virginia
- Bloomington, Indiana
- Columbia, Missouri (#6 in educational attainment)
- Bismarck, North Dakota (#10 in projected job growth)
- Fargo, North Dakota
- Lafayette, Indiana
- Iowa City, Iowa (#5 in educational attainment)
- Auburn, Alabama (#1 in projected job growth)

Top Metro Cities to Work — Best Areas for Business and Careers:

- Raleigh, North Carolina (#4 in projected job growth)
- Fort Collins, Colorado (#6 in educational attainment)
- Durham, North Carolina (#8 in educational attainment)
- Fayetteville, Arkansas
- Lincoln, Nebraska
- Asheville, North Carolina (#2 in cost of doing business)
- Des Moines, Iowa
- Austin, Texas (#8 in projected job growth)
- Boise, Idaho
- Colorado Springs, Colorado

This kind of research also allows you to uncover the areas of the country with the candidates and clients that need your services the most. Because Auburn, Alabama, is expected to have the biggest growth in jobs, the number of companies there searching for candidates will also be high. The area is limited in the number of candidates it can choose from to hire, so you can provide a service to the businesses in this area by helping them recruit candidates for their positions no matter where in the country the candidates live.

Market Area Research

Market is one way of referring to a city or a metropolitan statistical area (MSA). MSA is a term used in census research. Decide on a target city for your business. Start looking at various parts of the city. Focus on the parts that would be good for your business, which are detailed throughout the following pages.

Trade area research: Trade area refers to the area from which most of your customers will come. For example, if you specialize in placing legal professionals, you want to evaluate how many law firms, courts, mediation firms, and other businesses in the legal industry exist in the area where you want to open and operate your staffing business. If one or few client company options exist, you are not going to have many opportunities to fill positions for clients. If a dozen or more firms exist, you have more opportunity to get a law firm or legal business to hire you to help them fill positions.

Site research: After you narrow down your choices, look at the sites. Take pictures, make notes, and evaluate the various sites to determine which is best for your staffing business. If you intend to run a virtual office, you do not necessarily need to conduct site research. Instead, you will need to evaluate the area in your home in which you can set up your office with a quiet and professional environment.

Use the following list to evaluate a potential business site:

- Downtown area
- Historic district
- Business district
- Government offices
- Colleges/universities
- Technical schools
- Religious schools
- Military bases
- Hospitals
- Major highways

Evaluate these specifics about any location you are considering:

- How many similar staffing services are located in the area?
- Find sales volume (check business licenses for previous year) because business districts that have higher sales volumes have enough traffic

in the area for exposure of your business, and the businesses in the area might even be potential clients for your staffing business.

- Are there colleges or student housing in the area?

- What is the population of the immediate area?

- Is the population increasing, stationary, or declining?

- Are the residents of all ages or mostly old, middle-aged, or young?

- What is the median sales price and rental rates for area homes?

- What is the per capita income? This helps you to determine wage ranges in the area, which can help you set your fees and even negotiate salaries for placed employees when the time comes.

- Find the average family size. Population figures and household makeup help you to determine information about the candidate pool for the area in which you are considering opening and running your staffing business.

- Is the building and location suitable for a staffing or recruiting office?

Population and Demographics

Population and demographics are factors to consider when choosing your location. Places to obtain the details you need include the U.S. Census Bureau, **www.census.gov**, which supplies important information and statistics.

Demographics to evaluate include:

- Population density: The more people an area has, the more chances you have for identifying candidates who can fill the position your clients need you to. Areas with denser populations also tend to have more companies you can call upon to become your clients.

- Personal income: Income levels must be attractive enough to sustain locals or attract candidates from out of the area to relocate for a job.

- Age groups: If the population is primarily retired rather than of working age, you might not have much of an opportunity when it comes to finding local candidates. Especially if you are specializing or serving a specific geographic area, you want to focus on an area that has plenty of working-age candidates from which to choose.

- Employment statistics: Employment rates help indicate what is going on in your industry as it pertains to the area. Either a high unemployment rate or a low one can be opportunities for a staffing service.

A good source of information is the local chamber of commerce. To contact a chamber in another area, go to **www.chamberofcommerce.com**. You can get in touch with associations related to the staffing industry, such as the American Staffing Association or the National Association of Executive Recruiters (**www.naer.org**) to help you with economic and lifestyle patterns for your business research.

Your library and online sources can provide valuable information. Research librarians can help you. A website you should visit is DemographicsNow, at **www.demographicsnow.com**, to find out the market statistics in different areas of the United States. Statistics include average income, the number of adults, education levels of the people living in the area, and other demographic information that can help you identify an area as a viable business location.

Industry Information

For additional data and statistics, visit the following sites online:

The American Community Survey, **www.census.gov/acs**: Provides additional information from the supplemental census survey. This information covers demographics by county and MSAs. This survey is replacing the Census Bureau's long survey. It provides full demographic information for communities each year, not every ten years.

CenStats Databases, **http://censtats.census.gov**: This website provides economic and demographic information you can compare by county. The information is updated every two years.

County Business Patterns, **www.census.gov/econ/cbp/index.html**: Economic information is reported by industry, and the statistics are updated each year. Statistics include the number of establishments, employment, and payroll for more than 40,000 ZIP codes across the country. Metro Business Patterns provides the same data for MSAs.

Scouting the competition

Never underestimate the value of knowing your competition. Make a list of the other staffing services in your market whether your market is a geographic one or an industry specialty. If you are considering specializing in the finance and accounting industry, Robert Half would be a major competitor on whom you should conduct competitive research. Which ones target the same population that you will? Find out which types of staffing services they are selling and the prices they offer.

Take a detailed look at your competition when you narrow down your choices. The information you want can be hard to find. The best way to find information about your competition might be a visit to their establishments. Be creative. You will find if you contact competitors and tell them you are considering opening a staffing service of your own, many are more than willing to spend some time speaking with you or at least responding to your e-mail. Others are not. There is more than enough business to go around, and when staffing agency owners understand this, they do not feel threatened about providing tips and advice. If you do not feel comfortable asking directly, consider attending a networking meeting or chapter meeting that caters to staffing professionals in your area. You can gather information from the speeches and announcements and get the opportunity to mix, mingle, and speak with professionals working in the staffing industry.

Starting from Scratch

If you plan to start your business from scratch rather than buy an existing business or open a franchise, you will be on your own. However, your costs will be lower, and you will not have to follow the plans and policies of a franchise or deal with the reputation of a previous business owner. You will be in complete control and will have the prospect of success or failure on your shoulders. It will be up to you to find customers, market your services, research your vendors and potential partners, hire any employees, and set up your office. This is a huge challenge, but if you have a vision in mind, you might be eager to take it on. Planning is key.

Personality quiz

Business owners have personalities and tend to possess special characteristics you will not find in a standard employee. To evaluate whether you are ready to be a business owner, take the following personality quiz. The quiz helps evaluate whether business ownership is the most beneficial direction for you to take your career in staffing. Although you can be an exceptional staffing professional, placing employees and running a business of your own are two different things.

1. I am happiest when I am
    completely in charge of a project
    and use my own ideas................. ❑ Yes   ❑ Sometimes   ❑ No

2. I prefer to have a group of people
    brainstorm alternatives and
    then come to a consensus to set
    priorities and make decisions...... ❑ Yes   ❑ Sometimes   ❑ No

3. I like to have someone else with
    more experience set my targets
    and goals so I can meet or exceed
    them... ❑ Yes   ❑ Sometimes   ❑ No

4. I am excited about starting from
    scratch... ❑ Yes   ❑ Sometimes   ❑ No

5. I enjoy building teams as long as
    I am the leader. .... ❑ Yes   ❑ Sometimes   ❑ No

6. I feel uptight if someone asks
    me a question and I do not
    immediately know the answer. ... ❑ Yes   ❑ Sometimes   ❑ No

7. I enjoy pleasing the people I work
    for. .... ❑ Yes   ❑ Sometimes   ❑ No

8. I want to help my employees feel successful, and I know how to encourage others. .... ❏ Yes ❏ Sometimes ❏ No

9. My primary goals are to make a large amount of money fast and have leisure time. .... ❏ Yes ❏ Sometimes ❏ No

10. I like the idea of coming to work later in the morning and seeing my employees already working. . ❏ Yes ❏ Sometimes ❏ No

11. I know I do not know how to do everything, but I am willing to ask for advice and even pay for it. .... ❏ Yes ❏ Sometimes ❏ No

12. I would rather learn on the job by trial and error than pay for help. ❏ Yes ❏ Sometimes ❏ No

13. I would rather sit in my office making phone calls and setting appointments than working outside and sweating. .... ❏ Yes ❏ Sometimes ❏ No

14. I do not care whether I have to follow someone else's rules if I benefit from their expertise and make more money faster. .... ❏ Yes ❏ Sometimes ❏ No

15. I work and play outdoors. It is my favorite place to be. .... ❏ Yes ❏ Sometimes ❏ No

16. I hate being cooped up in an office. .... ❏ Yes ❏ Sometimes ❏ No

17. I have excellent mechanical skills. .... ❏ Yes ❏ No

18. I know I am good at what I do, but I know my limits. .... ❏ Yes ❏ Sometimes ❏ No

19. I am orderly by nature. I live by the motto: A place for everything and everything in its place. .... ❏ Yes ❏ Sometimes ❏ No

20. Even if my work area seems messy, it is organized to suit my needs. . ❏ Yes ❏ Sometimes ❏ No

21. I like the challenge of getting along with difficult people. .... ❏ Yes ❏ Sometimes ❏ No

22. One of my goals is to inspire others to succeed. I want to be a role model in my community. ... ❏ Yes ❏ Sometimes ❏ No

23. I would like a job at which I can get my hands dirty. .... ❏ Yes ❏ Sometimes ❏ No

24. I prefer the wilderness to a manicured golf course. .... ❏ Yes ❏ Sometimes ❏ No

25. I keep my checkbook balanced and promptly reconcile bank statements. .... ❏ Yes ❏ Sometimes ❏ No

26. I pay my taxes on time. .... ❏ Yes ❏ Sometimes ❏ No

27. I know the local regulations for the business I want to open. ....❏ Yes ❏ No

28. I feel comfortable negotiating prices with customers and vendors. .... ❑ Yes   ❑ Sometimes   ❑ No

29. I like to associate with people from different backgrounds. .... ❑ Yes   ❑ Sometimes   ❑ No

30. I will tell an employee the end result I want and let him figure out how to achieve it. .... ❑ Yes   ❑ Sometimes   ❑ No

31. I am rarely satisfied, and I always strive for improvement. .... ❑ Yes   ❑ Sometimes   ❑ No

32. I have always enjoyed working with numbers. .... ❑ Yes   ❑ No

33. I am willing to change any business practice or product at a moment's notice if I hear of something that might work better. ❑ Yes   ❑ Sometimes   ❑ No

34. I hate having someone else tell me what to do or how to do it. .... ❑ Yes   ❑ Sometimes   ❑ No

35. I am done with formal education forever. .... ❑ Yes   ❑ No   ❑ Maybe

36. I will ask customers for feedback regularly. If I do not hear complaints, I will not change anything in the business. .... ❑ Yes   ❑ Sometimes   ❑ No

37. I like to shop for bargains. .... ❑ Yes   ❑ Sometimes   ❑ No

38. I do not take chances; I plan for all possibilities. .... ❏ Yes ❏ Sometimes ❏ No

39. I can be fine without a regular paycheck for a while. .... ❏ Yes ❏ Sometimes ❏ No

40. I am eager to open this business. It is like a parachute jump — a leap into the unknown. .... ❏ Yes ❏ Sometimes ❏ No

41. I have enough of my own money and resources to start this business immediately. .... ❏ Yes ❏ Sometimes ❏ No

42. I know where to get more money if I need it. .... ❏ Yes ❏ Sometimes ❏ No

43. I am living paycheck to paycheck. I am tired of it. .... ❏ Yes ❏ Sometimes ❏ No

44. I want customers ready and waiting the day I open my doors. ..❏ Yes ❏ Sometimes ❏ No

45. I have many ideas about marketing my business, and I know how to get it done. .... ❏ Yes ❏ Sometimes ❏ No

46. I already have a company name picked out. .... ❏ Yes ❏ No

47. I already know which kind of customers I want to serve. .... ❏ Yes ❏ No

48. I dream about this business at night. .... ❏ Yes ❏ Sometimes ❏ No

49. I have a picture in my head of me
running my own business. .... ❑ Yes ❑ Sometimes ❑ No

50. My family and friends are
supportive of my business ideas. ❑ Yes ❑ Sometimes ❑ No

Scoring:

Business ownership might be appropriate for you if you answered yes on questions 1, 4, 5, 8, 12, 33, 34, 39, 41, 42, 48, 49, and 50. This response shows you have an independent spirit and are willing to take full responsibility for the job you are undertaking. A yes response on question 2 suggests you might want to form a partnership or at least consider bringing in employees, family, or other advisers to help you make business decisions.

A person well-suited to franchise ownership might answer yes to questions 3, 14, and 50. Someone who answers yes to 41, 42, and 44 might find purchasing an existing business more appropriate than starting from scratch. Yes answers to questions 18 and 30 highlight delegation skills.

A good attitude that will be helpful in business is demonstrated by yes answers to questions 11, 21, 22, 38, and 40. Yes answers to 15, 16,17, 19, 20, 23, 25, 26, 27, 28, 29, 31, 32, 37, 45, 46, and 47 show skills and affinities useful to business operation.

Finally, those who answer yes to questions 9, 10, 13, 24, 35, 36, and 43 might find the reality of business ownership difficult. This does *not* mean you cannot run a successful business just as a no to certain questions in the skills and affinities group does not mean you cannot succeed. But it *does* mean you might need to select partners or advisers or get some specific training to make the path of your business growth possible and realistic. It is always helpful to consider delegating work for an area in which your skills are not supreme. Also, showing your employees you are dedicated to doing the job will inspire them to make their best effort, too.

Franchises

Franchised businesses are individually owned businesses operated under the name and rules of a large chain, called the franchisor. The franchisor has perfected the successful path of running the business and has created a plan that the franchisees will implement. An entire program standardizes everything for you from start to finish. A service-oriented franchise, such as a staffing service, is a little more complicated. The customer is often buying from the franchisee because of his or her creativity, customer service abilities, and service mix.

The franchisor is selling the franchisee the right to operate a business using the company's name, logo, reputation, and selling techniques. And in the case of a staffing service franchise, the franchisor might sell a franchisee marketing rights to certain parts of the country, such as certain ZIP codes. This common practice eliminates competition among owners of the same franchise. This means the staffing service franchise would not be permitted to market its services in other parts of the country without the consent of the franchisor.

If you purchase a franchise, you will often purchase the franchise and a pay a percentage of gross sales on each sale you make. You might also be required to pay into a national marketing fund. The franchisor might require you to use certain vendors and might require you to purchase marketing materials from them. The franchisor is interested in brand consistency and image in the marketplace, and he or she might prefer you to use their marketing pieces or at least follow their marketing standards and guidelines.

Finding a franchise

There are various ways to find franchise opportunities. Use "staffing service franchise businesses" as search terms online. Go to the Franchise Opportunities website at **www.franchiseopportunities.com** and visit Franchise Gator at **www.franchisegator.com** to get information on franchised businesses and search for staffing service companies. *Entrepreneur* magazine annually gives a list of the top 200 franchised businesses and has many advertisements from franchisors trying to sell franchises. It even offers classified ads and display ads in the back of the monthly print issues of the magazine.

Another way to research franchise opportunities is attending a franchise exposition or conference at which the franchisors will be set up in the format of a trade show. Salespeople will be at the expo for the purpose of selling the franchise. Prepare yourself to attend the expo with only asking questions and obtaining information as your goals. Purchasing a business is a big decision, and you would not want to make a quick decision. To make the most of your expo experience, consider creating a list of questions similar to the following:

- How long has the company been in business?
- How many franchisees does the company currently have? How many are in your area?
- Is the area you would be interested in available? If not, which areas are available?
- What are the costs, including the initial cost to purchase the franchise, the royalties, and the marketing fees?
- How do the royalty fees work, and how long do you pay them?
- Are the royalty fees a percentage of sales or a set amount?

- What is the marketing fee?

- What assistance will the franchisor give you if you purchase? Is the assistance given just during the startup phase or on a consistent basis?

- How much control do you have as a franchisee over which types of staffing services you offer or how you run your business?

- Can you speak to an existing owner?

The franchisor will give you names and numbers of owners to contact, but also find others on your own to talk to. Be prepared to ask these owners specific questions to understand what it is like to own the business and work with the franchisor and the levels of sales you can expect. Ask for background information on the company, and do your own research to see whether this would be a good fit for you.

Investigating the franchisor

Request a copy of the franchisor's disclosure document, and review it carefully. The Federal Trade Commission has specific requirements for companies selling franchised businesses, and they require this document to be given to you at least 10 to 14 business days before you sign papers or pay any fees. This is done so you are not pressured into signing a contract and have plenty of time to review the document, talk with your attorney, and research what you need to do to understand the details of the deal.

The disclosure document, known as the Uniform Franchise Offering Circular (UFOC), is supplied to pre-qualified franchisees. They are available online, are about 50 pages long, and will include many details. If you go to the following website, **www.nasaa.org/content/Files/UniformFranchiseOfferingCircular.doc**, you will be able to view the entire document in Microsoft Word. It is supplied by NASAA, the North

American Securities Administrators Association. NASAA is an international investor protection organization. NASAA's form includes the following outline, and any UFOC should include this information:

- Franchisor name
- Business experience of key officials
- Litigation record
- Bankruptcy record
- Initial franchise fee
- Other fees
- Initial investment, including franchise fee, equipment, and any other costs
- Any requirements about where to purchase products and services
- Franchisee's obligations
- Franchisor's obligations
- Territories, including exclusivity and growth options
- Trademarks
- Patents, copyrights, and property information
- Obligation to participate in operating the business
- Restrictions on what the franchisee might sell
- Contract renewal, termination and transfers, and dispute resolution
- Earnings claims, or estimates of what the franchisee might earn
- List of all franchise outlets with contact names and numbers
- Franchisor's audited financial statements
- Receipt, or signed proof that the prospective franchisee received UFOC

- Use of public figures, including payment to celebrities or high-profile persons, and their investment in the system

This document will give you a comprehensive overview of the business, its stability, and the expectations of franchise owners. Study the expectations carefully because you will be bound by a legal contract to these terms.

Benefits of franchising

- **Growth:** They have created name recognition, which might help you quickly grow your business. Associating with a nationally recognized company might help when you talk to lenders for financing.

- **Experience:** You will be able to draw on the franchisor's experience and knowledge.

- **Consumer recognition:** Brand awareness and name recognition with both consumers and clients might give you an advantage and instant credibility.

- **Systems and marketing methods:** The company has designed a system that works and a marketing plan they supply to you. You are not starting from scratch.

- **Training and support:** They have proven techniques, and it is in their best interest to share these with you and train you to manage and promote the business. A good franchisor will be there to help you with all facets of the business.

- **National marketing:** You could reap the benefits of an ad that runs in *Metropolitan* magazine, for example, which you would not have been able to afford as an independent firm. This also sends a message to your customers that you are large and established. However, you must do your own local marketing and promotions.

These benefits are not a guarantee you will be successful; however, they will likely give you advantages over your competition.

Disadvantages of franchising

One of the disadvantages to opening a franchised staffing service is you will have to follow the company rules. You are not in complete control of your business. It will be the franchised name in the logo, not yours. There are other issues that you will have to accept with a franchise:

- You will be required to follow their standardized procedures and policies whether you agree with all them.

- You will share a portion of your gross sales with the franchisor. Gross sales encompass the total invoice value of sales before deducting customer discounts or returns. The portion you must share is a set percentage and is not based on your profit on a sale. This is an additional overhead cost, or operating expenses of a business, that an independent competitor will not have, and you have to consider this cost of doing business in your margin. In some instances, you must consider whether this will make your pricing less competitive.

- You might be required to purchase specific items from the company. If the company changes their name or logo, you will be required to purchase new letterhead, envelopes, business cards, and similar items.

- They might require approval of all your marketing, ads, promotions, and signs.

- The contract could be written to benefit the franchisor. This contract might set high sales quotas, give the company the right to cancel your agreement based on their criteria of what an infringement is, limit your ability to sell your franchise, and otherwise represent their best interests over yours. In this instance, if you have issues or problems with the franchisor, they will have more power.

- You can lose your franchise for breaching the contract. They can decide not to renew your contract, and if they do renew your contract, they might have the right to charge a new percentage on the royalty rate or impose other requirements.

- The contract might allow them to audit your books at any time, possibly at your expense.

CASE STUDY: FRANCHISE – FRIEND OR FOE?

Rhonda Chrestman, Owner
Taylor &Barnes Inc. d/b/a Snelling Staffing
499 Gloster Creek Village
Tupelo, MS 38801
(662) 842-1045
www.snelling.com/tupelo

In 1997, Rhonda Chrestman was the branch manager and selling manager for Manpower in Florence, Alabama. She was lucky and successful enough to land the account of a lifetime, which called for 400 temporary workers for three shifts. To fill the client's job order, Chrestman had to add three on-site coordinators, open an additional office, and finally add a Hispanic office to maintain the account.

About this same time, a Snelling Staffing franchise owner from Huntsville, Alabama, approached Chrestman. George Barnes had been an owner for about 25 years. He explained his interest in making Chrestman his partner and opening a Snelling franchise in a location that Chrestman could choose. Chrestman's mother had just been downsized as a human resource manager of a garment factory that was moving to Mexico. The two decided they wanted to work together and open a franchise.

Chrestman and her mom attended Discovery Day in Dallas, Texas, which is where the headquarters of Snelling Staffing is. Chrestman's mother spent one week and Chrestman spent two weeks at Snelling Staffing learning about and understanding the franchise operations. Both women found the Snelling family and the key management group were warm and possessed such a personal way of handling their business. This was much different than what both women were used to, and both were ready to get started right away.

George Barnes told the women of a program they could participate in that would eliminate the franchise fee, which could have been as much as $100,000. The arrangement would allow the women to use Barnes as a mentor. When they felt comfortable, they had the option to partner with Barnes by buying out his stock. About five years later, Chrestman and her mother bought Barnes out at about eight times the value.

Chrestman says one of the primary advantages of a franchise is the fact the franchisor is offering a business that is successful. The franchisor has already worked out all the kinks, offers free training, provides sales materials, provides hiring materials, has a legal team, provides safety and risk professionals, and provides everything you need to manage payroll and cash flow. The franchisor also offers all the back office support, such as W2 form preparation.

Name recognition was another benefit of running a franchise. Snelling Staffing turns 60 years old in 2011. People recognize the name, and many identify with the company. Chrestman says she has run across many hiring decision makers who tell her they or their parents or someone else they know landed their first job through Snelling.

Chrestman visited a Fortune 500 company that located a new plant in Tupelo, Mississippi. During her visit, she found out the company uses Snelling Staffing to find and place employees in other locations. This made it much easier to join their staffing team because they already trust Snelling in other markets. This is not an advantage a smaller staffing agency enjoys.

She says the primary disadvantage is you have to follow the rules and the decisions the legal team makes. These decisions often relate to whether to do business with a client. Chrestman found this to be frustrating at times but admits it probably saved her from working with some bad companies in the long run.

Chrestman worked with a company that basically closed down in the middle of the night and filed for bankruptcy but owed her staffing firm $275,000. One of the senior managers at Snelling Staffing called Chrestman and assured her they would work it out so she did not lose her business. Snelling Staffing loaned Chrestman the $275,000. Chrestman's franchise then paid back the loan in weekly installments. If Chrestman did not have a franchise, this one transaction probably would have forced her to close her business for good.

Chrestman says she advises everyone to buy a franchise instead of open their own business. She says losing focus is so easy when you do not have a plan that has been tested over and over and a team of professionals you can call anytime when you are in doubt or need an extra ear to help you make a business decision.

After more than 20 years in the staffing business, Chrestman's office has won numerous awards with Snelling. She won her Fast Start Award in 1997 when they opened the office, which is an award for the fastest growing office in the Snelling system. They are now WBEC certified, which means they are a woman-owned business, and are classified as a minority diversified vendor for the government and Fortune 500 companies.

Chrestman says opening a franchise was the best decision her mother and she ever made.

Franchise financing

The International Franchise Association (**www.franchise.org**) lists more than 30 franchise lenders in their Franchise Opportunities Guide. Also, the U.S. Small Business Administration (**www.sba.gov**) works with banks with guaranteed loan programs for beginning franchisees. Lenders have discovered the potential for growth and stability within the franchise market and are willing to look at financing these ventures.

Prepare a Business Plan

Business plans are your road map to success. The only way you can succeed with your business is by having a plan. It is at best difficult to establish and operate a business when you do not quite know how to go about it. Trying to accomplish it without a thorough assessment of what you want to accomplish, how you plan to go about it, and where you'll find financial support is also difficult. As you prepare to undertake the enormous task of starting a new business, evaluate your situation and visualize where you want to be three to five years from now. To work your way up to owning and operating a successful business, you must set goals to accomplish along the way that will serve as bench marks on your road to success. *A business plan specific to a staffing service is included in the accompanying CD-ROM.*

The most important and basic information to include in a business plan include:

- State your business goals.

- Describe the approach you will take to accomplish those goals.

- Discuss what potential problems you might encounter along the way and how you plan to address those problems.

- Outline the organizational structure of the business (as it is today and how you plan it to be).

- State the capital, or cash and goods you will use to generate income, to get started, and to keep your business in operation.

Various formats and models are available for developing business plans. Entire books are devoted to guiding you through business plan development. However, before you constrain yourself to any one business plan format, consider that business plans should be as different as the businesses for which they are being written. No two businesses are the same, and even though some basics might be similar, each business is as different as people are from each other. You should customize your business plan to fit your needs even though it is recommended you follow the basic structure of commonly used templates. A number of websites provide you with samples and templates that can also be used as reference, such as B Plans (**www.bplans.com**), NEBS (**www.nebs.com/nebsEcat/business_tools/bptemplate**), and PlanMagic (**www.planmagic.com**).

When writing your business plan, focus on its ultimate purpose and consider the reasons you are developing the plan and its possible applications. For instance, if you do not have a loan proposal, which essentially is a condensed version of the business plan for requesting financing, business plans can be supporting documentation to attach to a loan application. Plans are also used as a means of introducing your business to a new market or presenting your business to a prospective business partner or investor. *A sample business plan template is included on the accompanying CD-ROM.*

Parts of a business plan

Cover page

Align all the information on a cover page in the center. Always write the name of your company in all capital letters in the upper half of the page. Several line spaces later, write the words "Business Plan." Finish with your company's address, the main contact person's name, and the current date.

> NAME OF COMPANY
>
> Business Plan
>
> Address
> Contact Name
> Date

Table of contents

VI. Operations

VII. Strengths and weaknesses

VIII. Financial projections

IX. Conclusion

X. Supporting documents

Body of the business plan

MISSION STATEMENT

Present your business and what it is all about in the beginning of your business plan. A mission statement is only as significant as you intend it to be. It can be written somewhere and then disregarded as unimportant. However, it should be written and placed in important documents, such as this, and ultimately used as a beacon that will always guide you in the right direction. The mission statement addresses where you intend your business to go. When writing your mission statement, consider and discuss three key elements: the purpose of your business, the goods or services you provide, and a statement about your company's attitude toward your employees and customers. A well-written mission statement could be as short as one paragraph but should not be longer than two. *You can learn more about writing a mission statement in Chapter 12.*

I. EXECUTIVE SUMMARY

The executive summary should be between one and two pages long and should be written last because it summarizes all the information you have included in the plan. It should address what your market is, the purpose of the business, where it will be located, and how it will be managed. Write the executive summary in such a way that it will prompt the reader to look deeper into the business plan. Discuss the various elements of your business plan in the order you address them in the rest of the document.

II. DESCRIPTION OF PROPOSED BUSINESS

Describe in detail the purpose for which you are writing the business plan. State what it is you intend to accomplish. Describe your goods, services, and the role your business will play in the global market. Explain what makes your business different from all the rest in the same arena. Clearly identify the goals and objectives of your business. The average length for the proposed business description section is one to two pages.

III. MANAGEMENT AND STAFFING

Clearly identifying the management team and any other staff who might be part of the everyday operations of the business will strengthen your business viability by demonstrating it will be well-managed. A company's greatest assets are its employees. State who the owners of the business and other key employees with backgrounds in the staffing industry are. Identify the management talent you have on board, including yourself, and any others you might need in the future to expand your business. You might be starting with just yourself; however, in your plans for expansion, you might think about incorporating someone well-versed in recruiting professionals in a specific industry, such as finance. The management and staffing section of the plan could be as short as one paragraph if you are the only employee, or it could be as long as one or two pages depending on how many people you have and anticipate having as part of your staff.

IV. MARKET ANALYSIS

The market analysis section should include information on the different market areas you are considering covering in your business. For a staffing service, this might be geographic or industry-specific information. If you are new to the industry, include information you have acquired through research and data collection. Numerous sources of information are available online and in print that can provide you with a wealth of knowledge about the growth of the staffing industry, its resistance to recession, and its history. This process will add validity to your presentation, and you will be better prepared to answer any questions that might be presented to you. Essential elements to include in this section are a description of the types of staffing services you will provide, identification of your competition, and identification of what your planned strategy and approach are to the market. The market analysis element of your business plan should be one of the most comprehensive sections of the plan, and it can be several pages long depending on the number of products involved and the market you intend to cover. In particular, the portion of this section covering your target market can easily be two to three pages long.

Industry background

Rather than focus on the staffing industry in general, focusing on the background of the industry you intend to specialize in is better. For example, if your area of specialization is in the financial services industry, focus your description on staffing for this particular industry. If you are focusing your business on a geographic region, describe the staffing industry background as it pertains to the geographic region. In other words, alter your description so it pertains to your specific type of staffing service and your intended market. Include trends and statistics that reflect the direction the market is going and discuss how you will fit into that movement. Record major changes that have taken place in the industry in the recent past that will affect how you will conduct business.

Target market

This is one of the largest sections of the business plan because you address key issues that will determine the volume of sales and, ultimately, the revenue you will be able to generate for your business. Revenue is the total amount of money a company receives for its services. The target market is your customer, or groups of customers. By this point, you would have already decided on the role you will take on, so narrow your proposed customer base to a reasonable volume. If you try to spread your possibilities too thin, you might waste your time on efforts that will not pay off and miss out on some real possibilities. Identify the characteristics of the principal market you intend to target, such as demographics, market trends, and geographic location of the market.

Discuss which resources you used to find the information you needed on your target market. For example, state whether you used U.S. Census data or another source of statistical data. Elaborate on the size of your primary target market, or your potential customers, by indicating the possible number of prospective customers, their purchasing tendencies in relation to your placement services, their geographical location, and the forecasted market growth for that particular market segment. Include in your discussion the avenues you will use to reach your market, such as the Internet, printed media, and trade shows. Explain the reasons you feel confident your company will be able to effectively compete in such a vast industry. Discuss your strategies for globally competetive pricing, such as bulk discounts or prompt payment discounts. Some staffing services allow customers to pay invoices on a net 10 or 30 basis. If the service is placing

30 employees all as customer service agents, they might offer a discount to the client for their services because they can identify all these individuals with one set of search criteria. Finally, you must address potential changes in trends that might favorably or negatively impact your target market. *The CD-ROM includes a fee schedule agreement to have clients sign when using your services and a sample client invoice for billing.*

Service description

Do not just describe your service — describe it as it will benefit or fill the needs of potential customers, and center your attention on where you have a clear advantage. Elaborate on what your services are.

Market approach strategy

How do you anticipate entering such a vast market? Do you anticipate carving out a niche? Determining how to enter the market and which strategy to use will be critical for breaking into the market.

V. MARKETING STRATEGY

To operate a financially successful business, you must maintain a constant flow of income and boost your profits by increased sales. The best way to accomplish these is through an effective marketing program or plan, such as promoting your products and services through advertising, attending trade shows, and establishing a presence on the Internet. The marketing strategy element of the business plan identifies your current and prospective customers and the means you will use to advertise your business directly to them. This portion is likely to be several pages long, at least three to four, depending on how much detail you include. For a large, well-established business, it would probably be more appropriate to prepare a separate marketing strategy plan. However, for the startup, it would be appropriate to include the marketing strategy as part of the business plan. Even as part of the business plan, the marketing strategy section should include the following elements: products and services, pricing strategy, sales and distribution plan, and advertising and promotions plan. *The strategies are discussed in more detail in Chapter 12.*

Services

This section will focus on the uniqueness of your services and the ways your potential customers will benefit from them. Describe in detail which services your business provides, how the services are provided, and what differentiates the services from other businesses in the industry that provide the same service or deal with the same goods. Address the benefits of using your services instead of those of the competitors.

Pricing strategy

The pricing strategy segment is about determining how to price your staffing services in such a way that you remain competitive while making a reasonable profit. You will be better off making a reasonable profit rather than losing money by pricing your goods or services too high. Therefore, you must take extreme care when pricing your services. The most effective method of doing this is gauging your costs, estimating the tangible benefits to your customers, and making a comparison of your services and prices to similar ones in the market.

A good rule to follow is to set your price according to how much time you invest, and then add what you think would be a fair price for the benefits the customer receives. When you are determining your price for the goods or services, you must consider all the costs, such as those of running your office, selling, and administrating. In the staffing industry, you can use some standards as guidelines for setting your own fees. An executive recruiter charges as a placement fee 25 to 30 percent of the first annual salary of the candidate they place in a position. A temporary service firm, however, might charge 15 to 18 percent of the hourly fee for any temporary employees working for a client.

You should also address why you feel the pricing of your services is competitive. If your price is slightly higher than the competition's, you need to justify why you would still be able to move the service in the marketplace. Also point out the kind of Return on Investment (ROI) you expect to generate with that particular pricing strategy and within a specific time frame. ROI is a return ratio that compares the net benefits. In this case, the comparison is of the price of your services versus their total cost.

Sales

Now you have determined how to price your services, think about how you are going to sell and distribute your services. Describe the system you will use for processing job orders and billing your customers. Also, address which methods of payment will be acceptable from your customers, including credit terms and discounts.

Advertising and promotion

Discuss your plan for advertising your services through market-specific channels. This includes placing a display in the help wanted section of the local newspaper, creating and distributing fliers at the local college, and buying an ad in the phone book. Promote your business to a specific market. One of your goals in this section is to break down which percentage of your advertising budget will be spent on which media. For instance, the costs of advertising in trade magazines, at trade shows, and on the Internet differ significantly, and the return on your investment for each one of those might not be worth what you would spend. Therefore, it is wise to carefully evaluate your advertising and promotion plans before putting them into effect.

VI. OPERATIONS

The operations section covers all the aspects of management. Back all the information outlined in this section needs with realistic numbers, such as the costs of buildings, machinery, and equipment and salaries.

Discuss the current and proposed location of the business, and describe in detail any existing facilities. If you have employees, or anticipate having them, give a brief description of the tasks the employees will perform when processing the services and other duties the administration team will perform.

VII. STRENGTHS AND WEAKNESSES

As in most industries, numerous business owners are in the market competing for the same prospects. That business that can take better advantage of its strengths and work to overcome its weaknesses will get ahead of the game. In this section of the plan, elaborate on the particulars of your business that have enabled you, and will continue to enable you, to be successful. Discuss those things that set you apart and give you an advantage over your competitors, such as your location and your experience working in the staffing industry or the industry for which your business will specialize in providing staff. If you are skilled in multiple languages, you can work better business deals in several countries.

There are no strengths without weaknesses. As hard as it might be to face and deal with those weaknesses that could be holding you back, addressing them will help you to either overcome them or deal with them better. Having weaknesses is not a problem only your business faces because your competitors have weaknesses to deal with as well. Some weaknesses you might be dealing with at the time you write the business plan might be due to inexperience and limited exposure to the market, both of which you can overcome. However, some weaknesses you might have difficulty overcoming but must address head on include threats to your services from regulatory issues. Discuss each of the weaknesses you identify and the ways you plan to overcome them or foresee ultimately eliminating. Although important, discussing strengths and weaknesses should not take away from other focal points of the business plan. Therefore, keep this section to one page in length.

VIII. FINANCIAL PROJECTIONS

Financial projections are normally derived from pre-existing historical financial information. Even though your goal in this section is to address financial projections for your business, you should include some historical financial data that will help support your projections. If you are preparing a business plan as part of your business startup process, historical financial data will not be available. Working with estimates based on the performances of similar businesses will be acceptable. If you are using the business plan as part of the application process for a loan, then be sure to match your financial projections to the loan amount being requested.

When developing your financial projections, consider every expected and unexpected possible expense, but be conservative in your revenues. An expense is any cost of doing business resulting from revenue-generating activities. It is not critical your actual revenues exceed the estimated amount. However, it is not a good situation when expenses are more than expected. Your projections should be addressed for the next three to five years. Break down each year with the following information: projected income statements, cash flow statements, balance sheets, and capital expenditure budgets. An income statement shows a company's expenses and income or the difference between the two. A cash flow statement depicts where a company's money came from and how it was spent. A balance sheet provides a short explanation of a company's financial well-being; it contains the assets of a company, or anything under ownership of the business worth money; liabilities, including creditor claims working against company assets; and net worth, or total assets minus total liability. A capital expenditure budget outlines plans to fund acquiring or improving physical assets, such as buildings, property, or equipment. Due to the nature of this section, you can expect it to take up several pages of your business plan because you might want to include some graphs in addition to the budget forms to depict the information more clearly.

IX. CONCLUSION

The conclusion is the element of the business plan written last. Make use of this final opportunity to wisely state your case by highlighting key issues discussed in the plan. Close with a summary of your future plans for the expansion and progress of your business. Use language that will help the reader visualize what you will be able to accomplish and how successful your business will be if you receive the support you are requesting.

X. SUPPORTING DOCUMENTS

Attaching supporting documents to your business plan will strengthen it and make it more valuable. However, do not overburden it with too many attachments. Before you start attaching documents, ask yourself whether that particular piece of information will make a difference. If the answer is no, then leave it out. Documents that you should attach include:

- Copies of the business principals' résumés

- Tax returns and personal financial statements of the principals for the past three years

- Copies of licenses, certificates, and other relevant legal documents

- A copy of the lease or purchase agreement if you are leasing or buying space

- Copies of letters of intent from suppliers if applicable

Determine the Legal Structure of Your Business

The legal structure you would like to build your business under will be the backbone of your operation. The legal structure of your business will set the platform for your everyday operations because it will influence the way you proceed with financial, tax, and legal issues among others. It will even play a part in how you name your company because you might add Inc., company, or LLC to the end of the name to specify which type of company you are. It will dictate which types of documents need to be filed with the different governmental agencies and how much and which type of documentation you will need to make accessible for public scrutiny. Additionally, it will define how you will operate your business. To help you determine which way you want to operate your business, provided is a description of the different legal structures and a sample of documents you might need to file with state and federal agencies depending on where you live.

Business Entity Chart

Legal entity	Costs involved	Number of owners	Paperwork	Tax implications	Liability issues
Sole proprietorship	Local fees assessed for registering businesses are between $25 and $100	One	Local licenses and registrations and assumed name registration	Owner is responsible for all personal and business taxes	Owner is personally liable for all financial and legal transactions
Partnership	Local fees assessed for registering businesses are between $25 and $100	Two or more	Partnership agreement	Business income passes through to partners and is taxed at the individual level only	Partners are personally liable for all financial and legal transactions, including those of the other partners
LLC	Filing fees for articles of incorporation are generally between $100 and $800 depending on the state	One or more	Articles of organization and operating agreement	Business income passes through to owners and is taxed at the individual level only	Owners are protected from liability; the company carries all liability for financial and legal transactions
Corporation	Corporation fees vary with each state but can range from $100 to $500	One or more; must designate directors and officers	Articles of incorporation to be filed with state, quarterly and annual report, and annual meeting reports	Corporation is taxed as a legal entity; income earned from business is taxed at individual level	Owners are protected from liability; company carries all liability for financial and legal transactions

CASE STUDY: STRUCTURE IT THE RIGHT WAY

Frank Risalvato, Owner
Inter-Regional Executive Search Inc.
(IRES)
Charlotte (704) 243-2110
New York (973) 300-1010

Frank Risalvato started in the staffing business in 1987. In 1991, he started his own staffing service, IRES Inc. Over the years, IRES Inc. has gone through several "metamorphoses" ranging from a home-based startup, a single office, multiple offices from Albany through Charlotte at one time, and now back to a home-based business. This time around, however, the home-based business is more sophisticated than it was originally because it is virtual, which means the recruiters take advantage of streaming interviews and outsourcing of various roles.

IRES is an S corporation because at the time it was established, that was the best choice for maximizing tax deductions. According to Risalvato, this is still true, but he was told an LLC is slightly more advantageous for businesses starting from scratch today. According to the IRES Inc. CFO, a sub chapter S corporation was the best set up in 1991 because it eliminated the self-employment tax required by a C corporation.

The S corporation requires IRES Inc. to pay taxes on income at a personal tax rate rather than a corporate rate, which saves money. IRES Inc. thoroughly reviewed the possibility of changing to an LLC with the CPA. The CPA advised it would not be worth it for the company to close the existing business and start a new company to attain the LLC business structure. The CPA has extensive knowledge of the IRES Inc. situation and the personal situation of the owners and says this is the case.

Becoming a Small Business

A small business is a company with fewer than 500 employees. You will join more than 26 million other small businesses in the United States, according to the Small Business Administration (SBA). Small companies make up 99.7 percent of *all* employer firms in the country and contribute more than 44 percent of the total U.S. private payroll. More than half are home-based. Franchises make up 2 percent.

Of those 26 million small U.S. businesses, the SBA states that 649,700 new companies first opened for business in 2006. During the same period, 564,900 of the 26 million total closed shop. However, two-thirds of newly opened companies remain in business after two years and 44 percent after four years. The odds are with startups. Every company that survives does so because the owners are working hard and care about their company.

Sole proprietorship

Sole proprietorship is the most prevalent legal structure for startups or adopted small businesses, and it is the easiest to put into operation. It is a type of business one person owns and operates, and it is not set up as any kind of corporation. Therefore, you will have absolute control of all operations. Under a sole proprietorship, you own 100 percent of the business, its assets, and its liabilities. Some of the disadvantages are you are wholly responsible for securing all monetary backing, and you are ultimately responsible for any legal actions against your business. However, the relatively small expense to set it up is one advantage, and with the exception of a couple of extra tax forms, filing complicated tax returns in addition to your own is not a requirement. Also, as a sole proprietor, you can operate under your own name or you can choose to conduct business under a fictitious name. Most business owners who start small begin their operations as sole proprietors.

General partnership

A partnership is almost as easy to establish as a sole proprietorship with a few exceptions. In a partnership, all profits and losses are shared among the partners. A profit is the positive balance after expenses are subtracted, and a loss occurs when a company's expenses exceed revenues. In a partnership, not all partners necessarily have equal ownership of the business. Normally, the extent of financial contributions toward the business will determine the percentage of each partner's ownership. This percentage relates to sharing the organization's revenues and its financial and legal liabilities. One key difference between a partnership and a sole proprietorship is the business does not cease to exist with the death of a partner. Under such circumstances, a new partner can take over the deceased partner's share, or the partnership can be reorganized to accommodate the change. In either case, the business is able to continue without much disruption.

Although not all entrepreneurs benefit from turning their sole proprietorship businesses into partnerships, some thrive when incorporating partners. In such instances, the business benefits significantly from the knowledge and expertise each partner contributes toward the operation of the business. As your business grows, it might be advantageous for you to come together in a partnership with someone whose knowledge contributes in some way toward the expansion of the staffing business. Sometimes, as a sole proprietorship grows, the needs of the company outgrow the knowledge and capabilities of the single owner. This requires the input of someone who has the knowledge and experience necessary to take the company to the next level. In other instances, it becomes necessary to take on a partner because of the workload. Prefer to take on someone with a vested interest in making the company grow rather than simply earning a salary or commission for work performed.

When establishing a partnership, having an attorney develop a partnership agreement is in the best interests of all partners involved. Partnership agreements are simple legal documents that normally include the name and purpose of the partnership, its legal address, how long the partnership is intended to last, and the names of the partners. It also addresses each partner's professional and financial contributions, and how profits and losses will be distributed. A partnership agreement also needs to disclose how changes in the organization will be addressed, such as death of a partner, the addition of a new partner, or the selling of one partner's interest to another individual. The agreement must ultimately address how the assets and liabilities will be distributed should the partnership dissolve.

Limited Liability Company

A limited liability company (LLC), often wrongly referred to as limited liability corporation, is not quite a corporation but is much more than a partnership. An LLC has features found in the legal structure of corporations and partnerships. They allow the owners, called members in the case of an LLC, to enjoy the same liability protection of a corporation with the flexibility of a partnership for keeping records, such as not having to keep meeting minutes. In an LLC, the members are not personally liable for the debts incurred for and by the company, and profits can be distributed as members deem appropriate. In addition, all expenses, losses, and profits of the company flow through the business to each member, who would ultimately pay either business taxes or personal taxes but not both on the same income.

LLCs are a comparatively recent type of legal structure. The first was established in Wyoming in 1977. It was not until 1988, when the Internal Revenue Service ruled the LLC business structure would be treated as a partnership for tax purposes, that other states followed by enacting their own statutes establishing the LLC form of business. These companies are now allowed in all 50 states, and although they are easier to establish than a corporation, they require a little more legal paperwork than a sole proprietorship.

A structure like an LLC would be most appropriate for a business that is not large enough to justify assuming the expenses of becoming a corporation or being responsible for the record keeping involved in operating as one but is large enough to require a better legal and financial shelter for its members.

Regulations and procedures affecting the formation of LLCs differ among states. Visit your Secretary of State's website. You can find the information in the section for businesses. *A list of the states and the corresponding section of the Secretary of State's office that handles LLCs, corporations, and other entities is included in the Corporations section of this book.* Two main documents are normally filed when establishing an LLC. One is an operating agreement, which addresses the management and structure of the business, the distribution of profit and loss, the voting method for members, the process for handling changes in the organizational structure, and other such issues. Not every state requires the operating agreement.

However, every state requires Articles of Organization, and the required form is available for download from your state's website. The purpose of the Articles of Organization is to legally establish your business by registering with your state. It must contain, at a minimum, the following information:

- The LLC's name and the address of the principal place of business
- The purpose of the LLC

- The name and address of the LLC's registered agent, the person who is authorized to physically accept delivery of legal documents for the company
- The name of the manager or managing members of the company
- An effective date for the company and signature

For instance, Articles of Organization for an LLC filed in the state of Florida will look something like this:

ARTICLE I - Name

The name and purpose of the Limited Liability Company is:

Fictitious Name International Trading Company, LLC
Purpose: To conduct…

ARTICLE II - Address

The mailing and street address of the main office of the Limited Liability Company is:

Street Address: 1234 International Trade Drive
Beautiful City, FL 33003

Mailing Address: P.O. Box 1235
Beautiful City, FL 33003

ARTICLE III – Registered Agent, Registered Office, and Registered Agent's Signature

The name and the Florida street address of the registered agent are:

John Doe
5678 New Company Lane
Beautiful City, FL 33003

After being appointed the duty of registered agent and agreeing to carry out this service for the above mentioned Limited Liability Company at the location specified in this certificate, I hereby agree to take on the assignment of registered agent and will perform in this capacity. I further agree to adhere to all statutes and provisions associated with the proper and complete performance of my tasks, and I am knowledgeable with and agree to the conditions of my position as a registered agent as outlined in Chapter 608, Florida Statutes.

_____

Registered Agent's Signature

ARTICLE IV – Manager(s) or Managing Member(s)

Title	Name & Address

"MGR" = Manager

"MGRM" = Managing Member

MGR   Jane Doe
          234 Manager Street
          Beautiful City, FL 33003

MGRM   Jim Unknown
              789 Managing Member Drive
              Beautiful City, FL 33003

ARTICLE V – Effective Date

The effective date of this Florida Limited Liability Company shall be January 1, 2009.

REQUIRED SIGNATURE:

_____

Signature of a member or an authorized representative of a member

Corporation

Corporations are the most formal type of all the legal business structures discussed so far. A corporation is the most common form of business organization and is chartered by a state under its laws. A corporation can be established as public or private. Shareholders, or stockholders, own a public corporation, with which most of us are familiar. It is public because anyone can buy stocks in the company through public stock exchanges. Shareholders are owners of the corporation through the ownership of shares or stocks, which represent a financial interest in the company. Not all corporations start as corporations selling shares in the open market. They might start as individually owned businesses that grow to the point at which selling its stocks in the open market is the most financially feasible business move for the organization. However, openly trading your company's shares diminishes your control over it by spreading the decision-making to stockholders or shareholders and a board of directors. Some of the most familiar household names, such as the Tupperware Brands Corporation and The Sports Authority Inc., are public corporations.

A few individuals own a private corporation, and they are normally involved in the day-to-day decision-making and operations of the company. If you own a relatively small business but still wish to run it as a corporation, a private corporation would be the most beneficial legal structure for you as a business owner because it allows you to stay closely involved in the operation and management. Even as your business grows, you can continue to operate as a private corporation. There are no rules for having to change over to a public corporation once your business reaches a certain size. The key is in retaining your ability to closely manage and operate the corporation. For instance, some of the large companies that people are familiar with and tend to assume are public corporations happen to be private corporations. Domino's Pizza, L.L. Bean, and Mary Kay cosmetics are a few.

Whether private or public, a corporation is its own legal entity capable of entering into binding contracts and being held directly liable in any legal issues. Its finances are not directly tied to anyone's personal finances, and taxes are addressed completely separately from those of its owners. These are only some of the many advantages to operating your business in the form of a corporation. However, forming a corporation is no easy task, and not all business operations lend themselves to this type of setup. The process can be lengthy and put a strain on your budget because of all the legwork and legal paperwork involved. In addition to the startup costs are ongoing maintenance costs and legal and financial reporting requirements not found in partnerships or sole proprietorships.

To legally establish your corporation, it must be registered with the state in which the business is created by filing Articles of Incorporation. Filing fees, required information, and format vary among states. However, some of the information states most commonly require are as follows:

- Name of the corporation
- Address of the registered office
- Purpose of the corporation

- Duration of the corporation

- Number of shares the corporation will issue

- Responsibilities of the board of directors

- Status of the shareholders, such as quantity of shares and responsibilities

- Stipulation for the dissolution of the corporation

- Name(s) of the incorporator(s) of the organization

- Statement attesting to the accuracy of the information contained therein

- Signature line and date

For instance, Alabama's format for filing the Articles of Incorporation can be accessed through the state's Secretary of State Corporate Division website. The website contains instructions for filling out and submitting the document along with corresponding filing fees.

STATE OF ALABAMA

DOMESTIC FOR-PROFIT CORPORATION
ARTICLES OF INCORPORATION GUIDELINES

INSTRUCTIONS:

STEP 1: CONTACT THE OFFICE OF THE SECRETARY OF STATE AT (334) 242-5324 TO RESERVE A CORPORATE NAME.

STEP 2: TO INCORPORATE, FILE THE ORIGINAL, TWO COPIES OF THE ARTICLES OF INCORPORATION, AND THE CERTIFICATE OF NAME RESERVATION IN THE COUNTY WHERE THE CORPORATION'S REGISTERED OFFICE IS

LOCATED. THE SECRETARY OF STATE'S FILING FEE IS $40. PLEASE CONTACT THE JUDGE OF PROBATE TO VERIFY FILING FEES.

PURSUANT TO THE PROVISIONS OF THE ALABAMA BUSINESS CORPORATION ACT, THE UNDERSIGNED HEREBY ADOPTS THE FOLLOWING ARTICLES OF INCORPORATION.

Article I. The name of the corporation:

Article II. The duration of the corporation is "perpetual" unless otherwise stated.

Article III. The corporation has been organized for the following purpose(s):

Article IV. The number of shares, which the corporation shall have the authority to issue, is _____.

Article V. The street address (NO P.O. BOX) of the registered office: _____
_____,
and the name of the registered agent at that office: _____.

Article VI. The name(s) and address(es) of the Director(s):

Article VII. The name(s) and address(es) of the Incorporator(s):

Type or Print Name of Incorporator

_____
Signature of Incorporator
Rev. 7/03

Any provision that is not inconsistent with the law for the regulation of the internal affairs of the corporation or for the restriction of the transfer of shares can be added.

IN WITNESS THEREOF, the undersigned incorporator executed these Articles of Incorporation on this the _____ day of _____, 20_____.

Printed Name and Business Address of Person Preparing this Document:

Sometimes, finding the correct office within the state government's structure that best applies to your needs can be a challenge. The same office might have a different name in different states. In this case, the name of the office that provides services to businesses and corporations might be called Division of Corporations in one state, Business Services in another and Business Formation and Registration in another. The following is a chart of the appropriate office for filing Articles of Incorporation in each state.

State	Secretary of State's Office (specific division within)
Alabama	Corporations Division
Alaska	Corporations, Businesses, and Professional Licensing
Arizona	Corporation Commission
Arkansas	Business / Commercial Services
California	Business Portal
Colorado	Business Center
Connecticut	Commercial Recording Division
Delaware	Division of Corporations
Florida	Division of Corporations
Georgia	Corporations Division
Hawaii	Business Registration Division
Idaho	Business Entities Division
Illinois	Business Services Department
Indiana	Corporations Division
Iowa	Business Services Division
Kansas	Business Entities

State	Secretary of State's Office (specific division within)
Kentucky	Corporations
Louisiana	Corporations Section
Maine	Division of Corporations
Maryland	Secretary of State
Massachusetts	Corporations Division
Michigan	Business Portal
Minnesota	Business Services
Mississippi	Business Services
Missouri	Business Portal
Montana	Business Services
Nebraska	Business Services
Nevada	Commercial Recordings Division
New Hampshire	Corporation Division
New Jersey	Business Formation and Registration
New Mexico	Corporations Bureau
New York	Division of Corporations
North Carolina	Corporate Filings
North Dakota	Business Registrations
Ohio	Business Services
Oklahoma	Business Filing Department
Oregon	Corporation Division
Pennsylvania	Corporation Bureau
Rhode Island	Corporations Division
South Carolina	Business Filings
South Dakota	Corporations
Tennessee	Division of Business Services
Texas	Corporations Section
Utah	Division of Corporations and Commercial Code
Vermont	Corporations

State	Secretary of State's Office (specific division within)
Virginia	Business Information Center
West Virginia	Business Organizations
Washington	Corporations
Washington, DC	Corporations Division
Wisconsin	Corporations
Wyoming	Corporations Division

S Corporation

An S corporation is a form of legal structure. Under IRS regulations designed for the small businesses, S corporation means small business corporation. Until the inception of the LLC form of business structure, forming S corporations was the only choice available to small business owners that offered some form of limited liability protection from creditors and afforded them with the many benefits that a partnership provides. Companies operating under S corporation status are taxed similarly to a partnership or sole proprietorship rather than a corporation.

When operating under the S corporation legal structure, the business's profit or loss directly impacts the shareholders' taxes. The profits or losses the company experiences during a year are passed to the shareholders. They in turn must report them as part of their own income tax returns. According to the IRS, shareholders must pay taxes on the profits the business realized for that year in proportion to the stock they own.

The following requirements qualify an S corporation under IRS regulations:

- It cannot have more than 100 shareholders
- Shareholders are required to be U.S. citizens or residents

- All shareholders must approve operating under the S corporation legal structure

- It must be able to meet the requirements for an S corporation the entire year

Additionally, Form 253, *Election of Small Business Corporation*, must be filed with the IRS within the first 75 days of the corporation's fiscal year.

Electing to operate under S corporation status is not effective for every business. However, it has proved to be beneficial for a number of companies through many years of operation. Because of the significant role S corporations play in the U.S. economy, the S Corporation Association of America was established in 1996 to serve as a lobbying force in Washington to protect the small and family-owned businesses from too much taxation and government mandates. Membership in the association is composed of S Corporations, both big and small, from throughout the nation. This includes companies the Barker Company, a family-owned business that makes custom cases for refrigerated and hot displays found at supermarkets and convenience stores based in Keosauqua, Iowa. Another example is the Sumner Group, headquartered in St. Louis, Missouri. The Sumner Group is one of the largest independently owned office equipment dealerships in the nation.

After you determine how you want to establish your staffing service, you then need to consider the sources of financing for your business. *Chapter 6 covers the various costs and expenses of starting and operating a staffing service business.*

6

Financing

Before opening your staffing service for business, you first have to put all the pieces together to make it happen. The costs for starting and operating a staffing business vary according to the type of business and its location. *The evaluations you have to make to determine how much money you need to start the business are discussed further in the remaining chapters of the book, which cover costs of insurance, office setup and management, and others for running the business.*

Whether you end up needing $1,000 or $20,000 to get your staffing business off the ground, become familiar with the various sources of financing available to you that will provide you with the capital to successfully operate your business. Figures in a business's first operating budget are hardly ever concrete because you are only estimating expenses and revenue.

However, it gets easier each year. You get a better financial history to work with each year, and you can get close to accurately budgeting your revenues and expenses. The goal of this book is to provide all the tools and knowledge you need to open a business and to operate a financially successful one. You would not be a typical entrepreneur if your vision was not larger than the depth of your pocket. This is where establishing a sound budget and adhering to it come in to play. A budget is only as good as your ability to operate within it.

Financial Avenues to Take

Request financing for your new business through banks, commercial lenders, finance companies, and government agencies designed to help startups and small business owners. However, before you start looking at what your options are for requesting a loan for your business, first become familiar with the types of financing available. By knowing the differences between these types of financing, you will be in a better position to make an educated decision about what will best fit your needs.

Before you seek financial assistance

If you have all the money you need to start your business, you can skip this section for now. Eventually, you might need to find outside sources of funding to purchase equipment or supply working capital among other possibilities. The U.S. Small Business Administration suggests asking the following questions before seeking financial assistance:

- Is more capital needed, or are you able to manage current cash flow more effectively?

- How would you explain your need? Are funds necessary for expansion or as a cushion against risk?

- How quickly do you require assistance? By anticipating needs rather than searching for funds under pressure, you can obtain the best terms.

- How substantial are your risks? All businesses have risks, and the intensity of risk will affect cost and available financing alternatives.

- In which stage of development is your business? It is most essential to meet needs during transitional stages.

- What will the capital be used for? Lenders will stipulate capital be requested for extremely specific needs.

- What is the condition of the staffing industry? Depressed, stable, or growth conditions call for varying approaches to money requirements and sources. In times of decline, prosperous businesses will obtain better funding terms.

- Is your business seasonal or cyclical? Financial requirements for seasonal businesses are normally short-term. This depends on the types of candidates you place or the industry in which you specialize.

- What is the strength of your management team? Management is the key factor money sources considere. If you are a sole proprietor or are simply running the business on your own, it is your professional strength as a manager and business owner that counts.

- More importantly, how do your financing requirements mesh with your business strategy? If you are without a business plan, put writing one at top of your to-do list. All capital sources will request to view the business plan outlining the growth of your business.

Lending Institutions

You will have to choose from four different institutional lenders: commercial banks, credit unions, savings and loans, and commercial finances.

Commercial banks

A commercial bank is one of the most common forms of other people's money (OPM) that most people are already aware of or have used for a loan transaction. Some people will tell you bank money is OPM, but others will tell you bank money is your own money. This argument starts because they see borrowing money from a bank as borrowing against your own funds. For the purposes of this book OPM is considered any money borrowed to support your business plan that you would not otherwise have if you did not secure it from some outside source.

The general thought is commercial banking is the best place to get a business loan. One of the reasons is the Federal Deposit Insurance Corporation (FDIC) insures commercial banks, which have the largest selection among institutions with which a business owner can work. You also stand your best chances of getting a business loan through a commercial bank. A commercial bank stands to gain money from a successful business and will not turn away one that they feel will offer a minimal risk with the potential of providing a maximum gain. They are in business, too, and are looking for smart deals to take part in.

Commercial banks offer a variety of services that include checking accounts, certificates of deposit (CDs), loans, and fiduciary services for which they will hold something in trust and take responsibility for its care for another's benefit. They also accept pay drafts and can issue the business letters of credit when they are needed. Beyond these traditional loan services, today's commercial banks also offer credit cards and mortgages to further boost your chances of obtaining funds and allow you to spend those funds efficiently. The larger of the commercial banks are the better option for business. They can offer more perks, such as reduced fees, more local and national branches, and free ATM services no matter where you might travel.

When you are approaching a bank for the first time to ask for a loan, it is almost always better for you to start off with just what you need to launch the business or another relatively small amount. You might think your business is going to make you millions, but the bank will see the chances of this coming to fruition as slim to none.

Meet with the banker so he or she can tell you what you need to do to apply for and increase your chances of landing the loan. No ultimate manual can tell you everything about how to put together a package to present to the bank. Sometimes, the best ways to learn are through your initial mistakes and the gentle guidance of someone who is your bank ally. You might have to be rejected several times before you will understand how to get accepted. Also, the economy and business practices are fluid and change to keep up with current events.

Regardless of the business climate, the best thing you can do is conduct research and create a plan based on what is going on in your market at the current time. When preparing to approach a bank for a loan, be aware of different market types: low, high, recession, and recovery. No matter which market you are in, banks want to you to meet some basic guidelines. They do not engage in risky loans simply because it is not their business model. If you or your staffing business seems to be a risk, they are likely to pass regardless of the market. The following will increase your chances of securing a loan:

1. **Credit:** Banks follow a traditional pattern of loaning money. If they give you a loan, they expect to be paid back with interest, which is a fee paid on borrowed assets. They gauge your ability to pay them back by your credit history. If you have a history of paying back your debts, they will look more favorably at giving you a loan because you have a history of taking care of your financial obligations.

2. **Collateral:** If lending guidelines are tightening, consider offering something of value as collateral for the loan. This is a step to consider closely before going through with it, though. You need to ask yourself whether you would be ready to hand over your house or boat if the business were unable to repay the loan.

3. **Cosigning:** Depending on your credit history and any other factors a bank pulls into the equation, they might only feel confident giving you a loan if you have someone cosign the loan.

4. **History:** If you have a history of doing business with a bank, they might feel more confident working with you. Also, if you have a history of owning a business and can show a track record of success, they might also more easily extend a loan to your new staffing business.

The tighter the market, the tighter you might find a particular lender's guidelines to be. For example, in a recession, the reins of lending can be pulled in and loans be issued in a trickle. It might be difficult for anyone to get a loan — even those with excellent credit. Banks have their own goals and bottom lines to protect, and their guidelines will remain fluid to protect their own interests. Lending might become so lean you will have no choice but to seek OPM from untraditional means. *These will be covered in the rest of this chapter.*

The faithful banker plan

Institutional lenders are one of the most popular forms of traditional OPM, and they can become a strong ally to those with decent credit. Institutional lenders expect your full patronage and will work their best efforts for you if you satisfy all your traditional banking needs through one bank. Some banks can be like jealous best friends; they do not like you stepping out with other banks, seeing which kinds of deals you could get, and borrowing money here and there from a number of different sources. If you want a strong ally on your team, pick an institutional lender you like and stick with it. Of course, if a good opportunity comes along, you might want to try to work something out, but your relationship with your bank is like a marriage in that it is best when it is one-on-one without any third parties stepping in as temptation. Business is business, but you want to conduct smart business with long-term benefits; you do not want to burn any bridges as you grow your staffing business.

Advantages

❑ You can forge a strong relationship with a financial ally who knows you well.

Disadvantages

❑ The amount one bank might be willing or able to lend is limited.

❑ You might have high or variable interest rates that make the cost of the loan greater.

❑ It might take time to build a strong relationship.

❑ Your bank might close or be swallowed up by a larger bank, which would end your carefully honed relationship and leave you seeking a new one.

The "more the merrier" plan

Not all banks oppose sharing their customers with other banks, and if they know anything about smart business, they should probably expect to. The major branches have their own specialties and can offer large sums of money to good clients, but sometimes the smaller banks are more likely to do a deal that the bigger banks would shy away from. It is not a bad idea to have as many options at your disposal as possible.

Advantages

❑ It is a source for OPM when all others methods have failed.

Disadvantages

❑ You might have an interest rate that is high or variable.

❑ The amount the banks might be willing or able to lend is limited.

❑ It is still difficult for those with a bad or nonexistent credit rating to obtain money.

Credit unions

A credit union is set up as a nonprofit, and because of this, they tend to offer much better deals for their patrons. They are cooperative financial institutions in that they have members who have partial ownership in the institution. The earnings are divided among the members in the form of dividends or reduced interest rates. There are always exceptions, but it is common for a credit union to offer higher deposit rates and lower fees. However, to get these better deals, you will have to pay a membership fee and join the credit union by opening a savings account and buying into a share of the union. Only a member is welcome to deposit or borrow money in any capacity. This is what makes the credit union traditionally offer better rates and fees; it often has lower operating costs than the commercial bank and is content with much more modest returns.

Credit unions are not all the same, and most are not FDIC-insured. However, the National Credit Union Share Insurance Fund (NCUSIF) protects all federal credit unions and many of the state-chartered credit unions. The National Credit Union Administration (NCUA) administers NCUSIF. This is a federal agency responsible for chartering and supervising all the federal credit unions. Most credit unions offer the same services, such as checking and credit cards, as banks but do so under different terminology. For example, where a commercial bank uses the term checking account, a credit union calls it a share draft account. It is the same service but under a different name. But not all them will have the same services, and the ones that have more limited offerings will also not be as likely to offer the perks, such as convenient banking hours for those business owners who work long hours. The best thing to do is look around at the different credit unions available in your area and rate their services and fees compared with some of your larger commercial banks.

Savings and loans (thrifts)

Savings and loans, or thrifts, are similar to commercial banks in that they earn profit. Although most commercial banks can only branch by acquisition, the chartered thrift has more freedom and no limits in terms of waiting to find another bank they can acquire. It is cheaper for them to branch nationwide, which benefits the business owner with the lowest cost for services. However, one negative aspect of the federally chartered thrift is it limits the percentage of assets in a business loan to 20, a rule that remains in place as of the 2002 Office of Thrift Supervision regulatory bulletin.

Commercial financing

Commercial financing is basically a term to describe an asset-based lending system. In this system, the borrower is required to offer collateral in the form of personal or business assets, such as a home or other property. These assets are then used to secure the loan. The types of assets that you can gain financed include outstanding accounts receivable, certificates of deposit, bonds, contracts for import or export, purchase orders, existing inventory, major equipment, franchise development, and existing demand for product or service.

It is never too late to begin fostering a positive relationship with a bank, and here are a few steps you can take to accomplish this:

1. Know your bank manager personally, which means you are comfortable enough to invite him or her out to lunch or for coffee. Managers are more willing to go out of their way for someone they know than someone who has just walked in off the street. People conduct business with others they know and like.

2. Bankers are trained to recognize the signs of a snap business decision for the purpose of getting quick cash. They are not keen on such requests because they know the odds that any due diligence has been exercised to determine the feasibility of the business idea are slim. If you start building the relationship a few months before needing the loan and throw out occasional hints you might be in the market for a loan once you get your business plan solidified, it will greatly improve your chances of acceptance. The reason is they will know you have had time to consider your plan, and you are probably less risky than someone who has thrown something together quickly and is looking for some fast money to fund it.

3. Instead of selling yourself to the banker, try to have the banker sell him or herself to you. You want the bank to be aware you are presenting to them an opportunity to work with an up-and-coming entrepreneur and you are looking at other banking options. You are serious about your business and will be selective when you decide who will be your best ally during your climb up the mountain of wealth and success. To help turn the evaluation away from you and to the bank, try asking the banker several questions during your initial meeting. Such questions might be:

    + How long has he or she been with the bank?

    + Which types of clients has the banker assisted?

    + What is the bank's reputation in the business community?

    + Which type of criteria does the bank use for loaning to businesses?

    + What is the bank's Capital adequacy, Asset quality, Management, Earnings, Liquidity, and Sensitivity to market risk (CAMELS) rating?

Asking about CAMELS is basically asking the banker what his or her bank's safety and soundness rating is. This is something the banker might hesitate to give out because it is rarely made available to the public. Do not let that deter you from asking. It will show you are serious about finding a strong bank to build a good relationship with, not just obtain some quick cash from. Also, it will show you know what you are talking about because you have done your homework.

Another way to finance the start or growth of your staffing business is partner with one or more person for a specific purpose, which is known as a joint venture.

Joint Ventures

Sometimes, one of the best ideas for accessing a source of money is to partner with another business entity. This alliance between the two interested parties is not a merger because there is no transfer of ownership. Instead, it is a decision to share assets, knowledge, market shares, and profits. The companies involved are allowed to keep what is theirs, but they combine resources in a common interest to potentially create more profit than what they could generate individually.

Joint ventures have two primary functions: helping businesses learn new technology that will make them function more efficiently and giving them access they would not have otherwise had to new markets. If you are partnering with a large company that is interested in expanding in your operating area, this could mean you have just found a source of both OPM and other people's resources (OPR). A joint venture can be an opportunity if you are able to find the right company with which to align your company.

A joint venture can create a large business out of a small one. Sometimes, a small business can insert itself into a larger corporation in a market it would like to saturate. The larger business can profit through the small bussines's success while it can become a larger force in the market during a shorter period of time. Even small entrepreneurs have things to offer, such as an area of specialty, that a larger company might want, and convincing them of that will be as good as obtaining OPM from them.

One problem can occur when one of the companies is afraid to share its technology with a potential competitor and the other company is afraid to share its market area. If the businesses cannot find a measure of trust, they will not be able to give each other the support they need to ensure the success of the venture, which will cripple its potential. Also, a joint venture can mean you might lose a portion of the control you have over your business while you gain power and OPM within your business marketing area. In other words, you have to decide whether it is more important for you to own 100 percent of a $1 million company or only 10 percent of a $100 million company.

Not all joint ventures are created equal

Both parties must share equally for an initial agreement to work effectively. Such a plan is accomplished by checking the credentials of the other business. If both businesses can agree on a fair trade of services, this is well worth the effort. If the parties cannot agree, they will lose money and time, none of which a new business has the luxury of squandering, and ultimately defeat the initial intent, which is to strengthen their position.

The key to the acquisition of a successful joint venture arrangement is to find a need that a similar business might have. Determine how you could fill that need for them in a way that can be spelled out within a partnership agreement. Many joint ventures involve the combined efforts of two businesses targeting two different market areas.

As good as this can look on paper, it will certainly not fix everything for a new or stagnant business that is looking for an alternative market or technology. Do your homework to find a qualified, developed company to venture with, and your chances of success will go up exponentially.

The most important part of any joint venture, besides negotiations, is the contract. Every joint venture you consider must have an agreement so both parties know what is expected and which parameters will be involved. These are generally standard and straightforward agreements. They are fairly easy to come by on the Internet, but there are a few important aspects you will want to covere. The biggest concern is in which form payment will take. Will it be cash? Will it be part ownership of the business? Or is your business is producing a technology that the co-venturing partner might be able to use in return? Other aspects to consider include who will be responsible for making decisions and operating the business, who will be responsible for expenses, and under which terms the joint venture will dissolve.

Commercial and personal loans are not the only sources of funding you have to start and grow your staffing business. You can also turn to the federal government for some options on launching and expanding your business.

Federal Government

One of the primary federal government agencies that works with small businesses owners to boost success is the Small Business Administration (SBA), which was created in 1953. State and local government are supportive of small business ventures because they stimulate the economy for a region often by creating jobs. A small business that is a staffing agency creates jobs in two ways: by hiring its own employees and by placing candidates in positions with other companies. Despite complaints people have about the government and taxes, they can learn to take advantage of the money they have put into the government and let it work for them. The SBA has become a big help because the government has realized its best chance of getting a return is through funding small business programs.

The SBA is not the source for your loan but coordinates the loan with a participating bank or institution. When an institution sees a business as unfit or too big of a risk, the SBA will step in and make as large as a 90 percent guarantee to the bank it will pay off the loan regardless of what happens to the business. This guarantee makes banks friendlier to deal with, especially if you are getting used to being turned down. These loans are not handed over to just anyone. The entrepreneur must prove through an extensive application process they will be able to pay off the loan and have collateral to back it up.

The SBA loan is a good option because its terms as more favorable than what you might find with conventional bank financing. SBA programs do not require a large down payment, whereas 20 to 30 percent is common for the conventional lending institution. The typical down payment for an SBA loan is 10 percent, and it has the ability to offer an amortized term of up to 25 years. The SBA also does not carry **balloon loans** that will drop a large bomb on the business once the loan has reached maturity.

Small businesses fall prey to the balloon loans because they are initially attracted to the relatively low payoff amount over the course of the loan. This can be beneficial for managing the cash flow of the business. The problem is they would be forced to refinance and incur the penalty of several fees on top of their balloon payment if they did not save up for it by the end of the loan. With the typical loan amortization, the time between the initial loan and final judgment day is within five to ten years, which can be a delicate time for most new businesses.

The SBA helps keep money accessible to the small business so it does not deplete all its own capital, which could potentially stifle the business's growth. These loans are also compatible for moderately small corporations. They offer loans up to $2 or $5 million. This will not be sufficient for a Fortune 500 company that works with multimillion dollar loans; these programs were not designed for the big guns that small businesses have to sometimes compete against. However, these loans can help level the field. Eight popular SBA programs are available today. To begin with, talk to your bank about applying for a loan through the SBA. You need to supply your bank lender with any paperwork, such as financial statements and your business plan, they request to submit a loan application. If the bank is unable to extend you a loan, ask them to consider your loan under the SBA's guaranty program. Be familiar with the details of all eight of the SBA's programs.

Basic 7(a) Loan Program

This is the SBA's primary business loan program. Although its maximum allowable loan is $5 million, it is the most flexible in its terms and eligibility requirements and is designed to accommodate a wide variety of financing needs. Most of these loans are given to provide working capital or fund machinery, equipment, furniture, renovation, new construction, and debt refinancing. Commercial lenders are the ones who make the loans and determine who they will loan to, but the government offers a guarantee for a percentage of the loan should the borrower default or fail to meet the terms of the loan. For this particular loan program, the government can guarantee up to 75 percent of the total loan if it exceeds $150,000 and 85 percent for loans less than $150,000.

The most attractive features of the 7(a) are its low down payment, low interest rates compared to most banks, and an extended loan maturity for as many as 10 years for working capital and 25 years for fixed assets. Should a business want to start an early payoff, a small percentage of the prepayment amount will be charged as a prepayment fee. The early payoff can come in handy when a business is experiencing fast growth and needs to refinance to support its expansion, and the small fee required to do this might be more worth paying.

Microloan Program

This short-term loan offers up to $50,000, to small businesses that are starting up or growing. Funds are made available to intermediary lenders who are nonprofit and community-based, and these lenders require some form of collateral for the loan. The loan can be used as working capital to fund the operations or to purchase inventory, supplies, and equipment do business or furniture and fixtures for the business. There are intermediaries available in most states, the District of Columbia, and Puerto Rico. The states in which there is no intermediary include Alaska, Rhode Island, Utah, and West Virginia; Rhode Island and a section of West Virginia are currently accessing intermediaries in neighboring states.

Prequalification Pilot Loan Program

This program allows a small business to have their loan applications analyzed and receive a potential blessing from the SBA before a lender or institution considers the application. It covers loan applications for which the business owner wants up to $250,000, and its deciding factor involves aspects of the applicant's credit, experience, reliability, and character to some degree. This makes it different from many of the other loans for which the applicant must have assets to be qualified.

The main purpose for the SBA in this particular program is to help the entrepreneur strengthen his or her loan application. This program can be helpful for an applicant who has relatively good credit and a semiestablished business looking for expansion. The SBA will ask to see the applicant's financial records, ratios, history, and personal credit. The SBA will help determine which sections of the loan request are potential red flags for the bank and then recommend the most favorable terms the applicant should expect.

8(a) Program

This program was specifically designed to help socially or economically disadvantaged people, such as minority entrepreneurs, minority business leaders, or people with disabilies. These loans are traditionally used for a startup or business expansion. To qualify, a socially or economically disadvantaged person must own and control at least 51 percent of the business and cannot be a figurehead. Along these same lines are additional assistance programs that are specifically targeted to veterans, women, and handicapped persons.

Economic Opportunity Loans (EOL)

This program is for the low-income business owner who might be experiencing difficulty securing financing despite having a sound business idea. An applicant can qualify for EOL assistance as long as one business partner is living below the poverty level determined by the federal government and adjusted annually for inflation and owns at least half of the business. It is also an option for the small business that has already been declined by a conventional bank or institution. The best part of the EOL program is the loans are long-term and can be paid back in 10 or 25 years depending on the type of loan.

LowDoc Program

The LowDoc, short for low-document, Program is set up to make the application process much simpler, less time-consuming, and quicker. It does this by reducing the size of the application form to one page for loans under $50,000. For larger loans of $50,000 to $100,000, an applicant receives the same one-page application along with a request for his or her pervious three years of income tax returns. This program is the most popular in the SBA's history.

CAPLines

A CAPLines loan is an asset-based line of credit that allows businesses to manage their short-term needs, such as to pay employees and purchase equipment. A business, such as a builder or small company, that is unable to qualify for other lines of credit will use this type of loan. The terms to pay back a CAPLine are adjusted to fit the seasonality and cash flow of a business, for example when a business has completed a large project and is waiting for payment.

SBA lenders are not all created equal. They are separated into three categories, and each category participates in the programs with different verve and commitment. The least helpful in most cases will be your participant lenders.

- **Participant lenders** are occasional participants in the programs the SBA offers. This is the status of your average bank. They are known to process slowly and are often impersonal. The SBA also does not entirely trust them to determine an applicant's qualifications. For this reason, the SBA checks over each application and will have the ultimate say on whether the applicant meets requirements for the loan.

The next best SBA lender to use would be the certified lenders.

- **Certified lenders** are considered certified because they are regular participants of the SBA programs. Processing time for these loans is shorter because certified lenders are more accustomed than participating lenders to the processing. Although they understand the SBA process better and complete the necessary requirement checks, the SBA still insists on double-checking the decisions of the bank before qualifying the loan.

The best type of SBA lender is the preferred lender.

- **Preferred lenders** know the SBA system and have a solid reputation with the SBA as a good judge of character and risk. Because of their experience, the SBA trusts them and does not get involved in the decision-making process of acceptance. If the bank accepts the applicant, the SBA is 100 percent behind the decision. This is the quickest and most convenient way to take out an SBA loan.

Grants

So far, this book has talked about the many forms of government funding that have to be paid back. What if there were a way to dodge this aspect of borrowing money? For some businesses, there exists just such a tool, known as the grant. Grants exist because things need to get done, which requires people to carry out the work. They tend to go to projects involving people helping others, and the money is intended for a specific purpose. You will need to meet the conditions the grant giver mandates and then use the funds for the mandatory purpose. Grants must be applied for. You respond to a Request for Proposal (RFP) and follow the criteria that has been issued for which types of information the organization offering the grant needs to reach its decision. Proposals are reviewed, and the grant money is awarded to the winner(s).

Although the federal government is not as generous with its use of grants for most small businesses, many local state governments are. About the only small businesses eligible for a grant these days are research firms in engineering and science because these are capable of serving the needs of the country. These grants are through the Small Business Innovation Research Program, and you can find more information online (**http://science.energy.gov/sbir**). According to the website, its motto is, "Supporting scientific excellence and technological innovation through the investment of federal research funds in critical American priorities to build a strong national economy… one small business at a time." Government entities recognized small businesses were engaging in more innovation than bigger businesses but the funding had been tilted in favor of those larger companies. This program helps level the field so small businesses are able to compete and continue to innovate.

Beyond these few financing entities that answer the need of the federal government, the small business can find yet another ally closer to home than they might have realized: their local state government. Every state has its own rules and privileges, so you will need to contact your state's economic development center. Research its website to see what it offers.

Government grants are created to fulfill specific purposes and can have narrow qualifying requirements. You might not find a government grant you can fulfill, or you might not be able to fit within its stringent guidelines. But the government is not the only entity that offers grants. In addition to government grants, there are three more types of grants: foundations, corporations, and individuals.

1) **Foundations:** An alternative to government grants is available through the private sector via foundations. About 100,000 foundations might be interested in what you do and might be willing to provide you with the cash to bring your idea to fruition. For example, if your business idea involves an eco-safe cleaning service, there might be an eco-friendly foundation that would be

willing to offer you a grant. For more information on foundation grants, go to **www.foundationcenter.org**.

2) **Corporations:** Many companies set up programs in which they offer grants or will match money for the development of products and services in their industry. They also sometimes offer their expertise or equipment or other resources. They offer grants to nonprofit organizations within their community to show support for local causes. If your business idea is to establish a nonprofit organization, look around your community for existing businesses that are already involved in the type of outreach programs that align with your idea.

3) **Individuals:** Generally, wealthy philanthropists set up foundations through which they issue grants. It will depend on whether your business idea strikes a chord with someone interested in what you are trying to accomplish, especially if your endeavor is civic-oriented. Individual grants are competitive, and the guidelines for what the grant providers want done with their money can be specific. So, if you cannot find any grant opportunities through the government, foundations, or other corporate entities, an individual philanthropist could be a viable option.

Other Ways to Finance a Business

1. Giving: Contributions can serve as a primary source for business financing.

2. Borrowing: Other ways you can borrow money.

3. Selling: Even though selling a part of your business to investors might bring in much needed capital, sharing this portion can cause difficulties.

4. Earning: The most effective way to promote growth is to manage money wisely and save calls for long-term planning.

5. Pledging: Depending on efforts to give back to the community, development grants could be accessible for public or private businesses.

6. Sharing: Team up with a sponsor, employer, business, or individual who will agree to fund your idea to come closer to reaching their own ultimate goal.

Examining your business and discovering your entrepreneurial style are the first steps to finding the funding that matches your company's needs. When the need for money arises, entrepreneurs can become consumed by raising capital. Their judgment becomes clouded and their decision-making ability compromised. Your first step to exploring your financing options is to determine what you are willing to sacrifice.

Available financing sources

The following overview discusses the types of financing available to businesses. Making the decision to start or expand a small business opens up a variety of considerations and options. Many burgeoning companies spend far too much time chasing down funds from sources that do not mesh with their business. Making the right deal with the right investors or lenders provides you with the opportunity to grow in a manageable and hospitable environment. Making the wrong deal with the wrong investors can cause serious problems down the road; it can set you up for conflicts and even potential failure.

Give it: Your personal investment

Investors and lenders will expect you to provide a significant amount of the capital necessary to launch or expand your business. Putting your assets on the line sends the message you are committed to making the company a success, which makes it easier to acquire supplemental funding from outside sources. There are a few exceptions, such as seed money programs created to help economically disadvantaged, at-risk individuals. It is recommended you have enough money saved to live off of for three years because your business most likely will not make a profit in the first year or two.

Investing your money

Nearly 80 percent of entrepreneurs rely on personal savings to begin a new enterprise. Using personal savings secures the entrepreneur's control and ownership of the business. Because it is your money, no debt is incurred and future profits are not shared with investors.

Converting personal assets to business use is the same as giving your business cash. You will avoid purchasing these items and be able to depreciate them. Your accountant will set up the conversion and depreciation schedules. For many people, their greatest personal asset is their home.

Lines of credit, refinancing, and home equity loans are often used. Raising cash this way can be risky. Personal credit cards, signature loans, and loans against insurance policies and retirement accounts are other common ways of raising startup capital.

Home equity loans

You will need to know the equity you have in your home. For less than $500, an appraiser or real estate agent can locate home sale comparisons for you to use as an estimate.

If you own your home, you can refinance without staking all the equity you have in your home. This leaves room for future refinancing should something go wrong. You should not consider borrowing against 20 percent or less in equity. The funds you gain will be minimal, and the second lender will not hesitate to foreclose should trouble arise.

The best way to determine feasibility is to follow these steps:

1. Get your home appraised. If the value has gone up, you might own more equity than you think.

2. Figure out exactly how much you still owe on your mortgage.

3. Take the appraisal valuation and subtract your debt to determine the amount of equity.

4. Figure out your percentage by dividing your equity amount by the valuation amount. If it is less than 50 percent, you should find a different source of capital for your business.

5. If your equity is more than 50 percent, you might be in business. Now is the time to get loan quotes.

6. Figure out how your business plan will be affected by this cash infusion, and make projections for how long it will take to pay off the loan.

Pay down the principal balance of the debt to get out of debt faster and regain the equity on your home.

Leveraging your credit

Leveraging your personal credit worthiness is another way to support your business. A new business has no established credit. Your signed personal guarantee will help establish credit for your business. Ask your attorney about personal liability issues for all business debts. Protecting your personal credit and financial health is a key reason to incorporate.

Borrow it: Loans to repay

Borrowing can either rescue your business or act as a burden to your company. When researching different types of loans, keep in mind such issues as collateral required, interest rates, and repayment terms.

Loans from family and friends

When searching for capital, a smart move would be to ask those who are close to you for assistance. Because you have established a relationship with your family and friends, they will not question whether to trust you, and a desire to help will already be present.

Instead of the bank, friends and family can offer to help start up a business by providing interest-free or low-interest loans. This way, control is in full hands of the business owner.

When considering these investors, ask yourself five questions:

1. Will this person panic about money after investing?

2. Does this person understand the risks and benefits?

3. Will this person want to take control or become a nuisance?

4. Would a failure ruin your relationship?

5. Does this person bring something to the table besides cash that can benefit you and your company? If he or she does, you might be able to leverage his or her knowledge and skills to help boost your business above what a monetary contribution would provide. If not, contributing the money might be the way he or she can best benefit your business.

Credit Lines

Many small businesses are drawn to microloans. These loans provide a short-term borrowing option and are safer because they have lower rates of interest. Microloans can help close the gap between manufacturing costs paired with delivery and the time needed to receive full payment from customers. Credit lines help meet payroll.

Sell it: Shared ownership

Investors are a type of owner, which means you must be willing to sell a portion of your business and future profits. Some investors are active participants in daily operations while others offer guidance and support through board meetings. Still, others prefer to let you do it all while they reap the rewards.

Earn it: Creative ways to earn cash

Some entrepreneurs have discovered untraditional ways to launch or expand a business. Networking with other entrepreneurs and locally established businesses is an excellent way to find creative solutions to financing your company. Here are some ways other entrepreneurs have earned cash and discounts.

Saving

Trimming costs, taking advantage of banking discounts and rebates, and starting a business savings account should have first priority. Make regular deposits to start your future.

Buying groups

These groups maximize vendor and supplier discounts and reduce costs for entrepreneurs needing everything from office supplies to raw materials. Some are free while others require a membership fee. Some of the primary examples for business group savings include wholesale warehouses, such as Sam's, BJ's, and Costco. Each of these membership programs offers business memberships and provides discounts on items and programs that pertain to business owners rather than individuals. Savings include business services, such as accountants and lawyers, or business software.

Competitive awards

There are local, state, and national contests in which companies compete for financial and support awards based on technological advances, excellent customer service, and hiring practices. Contact the business office for your county and state to find out more information on awards you might be eligible to apply for. Also, contact the local chamber of commerce for information on organizations and businesses in the area that provide these types of financial awards in your community.

Pledge it: Good for the whole community

Private organizations and public agencies give money to businesses because the businesses are performing some sort of good will that benefits the community Their helping hand can come in the form of one of the following:

- Direct grants that require no financial repayment

- Grants that are repaid from future revenues but do not have to be repaid if your business fails

- Economic development programs that are designed to maximize your business's financial impact on the community

- Location grants that offer a financial incentive to locate or move your business to economically stimulate a community, city, or state

- Soft loans that offer less stringent qualifications and softer terms and conditions, such as no interest or low interest

- Tax cuts, deferrals, and deductions that lower your business, personal, or property taxes

- Subsidies that pay for a portion of the cost of approved services when you actively promote your use of the services

- Support in the form of free advice and access to resources that saves you consultation fees and improves your chances for success

Some ways you can give back to the community are to set up your business in an economically depressed area, to hire special needs or high-risk employees, volunteer in your community, or mentor others. The financial benefits for your company and your community can be substantial. In addition, being a good citizen never hurts your company's brand and community image.

Credit card financing

When used carefully, credit cards can supply supplemental or emergency cash flow. The buy now, pay later philosophy can work well for businesses that might not have the capital needed to pay bills but expect to soon. Many businesses will try to finance their entire operation using personal and business credit cards. It is not recommended. The interest rates are high, and once you have reached your limit and you no longer have adequate cash flow, you could be out of business.

Using a personal credit card to help fund a business is a viable option that thousands of companies use. Instead of using a personal credit card, however, it is better to use a business credit card account. Once you have established your business, you will notice scores of credit card offers. Banks that would never give a small business a loan for $100,000 will extend a $100,000 credit line to the same small business. The interest rates, anywhere from 5 to 25 percent, are much higher. The rates are rarely fixed, and if you fall behind on payments, they rise immediately. Using a business credit card keeps your personal and business finances separate, which is easier for budgeting, expenses tracking, and filing tax.

Still, these interest costs are often lower than the bank's loan fees, which drives many businesses to use credit cards in lieu of bank loans. This extends the time it takes to pay off the credit card and saves money by swapping for another card with a better interest rate. Credit cards should be used primarily for fast capital that will be repaid after a short amount of time. The longer it takes you to pay off the existing balance, the more the money you borrowed costs you.

Credit cards can be advantageous and disadvantageous for companies. When handled correctly, they can supply a great deal of emergency and short-term funding sometimes less expensively and more easily than other sources of capital. Using them incorrectly can cause the business to suffer and irreparably damage the founder's personal credit history.

To sum up, the good points of credit cards include:

- They are easy to obtain.
- The lines of credit can be as high as $100,000.
- They are accepted almost everywhere.
- The money is immediately available for emergencies.
- The incentive programs, such as frequent flyer miles, can save money on other expenses.
- There is little paperwork and no extensive forms to complete.

The bad points include:

- The interest rates can be as high as 25 percent.
- Interest rates are not locked and will rise considerably if you fail to make minimum monthly payments.
- Many cards have hidden fees, which makes them more expensive.
- Mismanagement of cards can ruin your personal credit.
- Having to make monthly payments on cards and for other loans can cause huge cash flow problems for your business and force it into a cycle of debt.

Writing a Loan Proposal

Successfully securing a loan for your business takes some work on your part because the more prepared you are, the better your chances of a favorable outcome. When you approach a lending institution to request a loan for your business, you need to state your need clearly and provide all the required supporting documentation of the financial situation of your business. Therefore, the best and most professional way to present your request is by preparing a loan proposal.

A loan proposal is a condensed version of your business plan because you want to provide the lending institution with enough information for them to make an informed decision on your loan. The information must be concise yet adequately present a full picture of your business and contain all the critical information. It must be a professional document with up-to-date information on your staffing business, including any possible changes in the company in the near future. In addition, you should explain any terms or technical information that might not be common to someone outside the industry because not all individuals who are going to be reviewing your loan proposal are knowledgeable about the staffing industry.

When working on your financial projections for your loan proposal, try to be conservative in developing your revenue estimates. Extremely high revenues might seem unrealistic and out of reach. On the other hand, when estimating expenses, make sure you consider all possible costs and avoid underestimating because you do not want to run short of funds earlier than anticipated. To avoid any questions on the validity of your numbers, it is good practice to include a narrative explaining how you arrived at the figures for both your revenues and your expenses.

A solid loan proposal will include a written narrative of the fundamental aspects of the project for which you are seeking the loan, relevant financial information, and all necessary supporting documentation, such as the Articles of Incorporation or other business entity documents. Each lending institution might have different requirements for submitting an application for a loan.

Professional Advisers

For many business owners who are not involved in a partnership, one of the more frustrating aspects of being the boss is not having someone to bounce ideas off of or someone above you to ask for help. The Small Business Development Consultants are one avenue to outside advice. Although they are there to serve your needs, they are also serving the needs of dozens or hundreds of other business owners.

You will want to create a personal network of business advisers, including those with professional credentials. The sooner you can bring experts onto your business team, the better for both you and your fledgling business. Be sure to include these professionals on your short list of necessary advisers:

- A **certified public accountant (CPA)** or someone of equal ability in accounting. You will need this person to provide advice and services for local, state, and federal taxes; loan terms; and other business expenses. A competent accountant can show you how to get the most profit for each dollar of income. He or she might even have good ideas for additional sources of income for your business. If you do not know a good accountant whom you trust, get firsthand referrals from a successful business owner or banker.

- A capable **business attorney**. Build a relationship with a good business attorney so you always have someone knowledgeable on hand to go over a contract to look out for your special interests, give legal advice in hiring situations, or advise you on legal forms and requirements at your state and local levels. You will want someone experienced. It is not good for you to be the guinea pig for a startup attorney even if you are running a startup yourself.

- A **business banking expert** from your primary business bank. You want a banker who is interested in the growth of your company — who is literally banking on your success. A good business banker can help you network with vendors or even find new customers. Often, the business banker has a deep reservoir of business knowledge that he or she would like to share with you, so ask questions.

- A solid business insurance agent or broker. A broker might be your wisest choice because he or she theoretically will check out several different insurance companies for you and recommend only the one he or she believes is best. Look to a professional insurance adviser to help you analyze and prepare for your business risk.

Perhaps you do not want to deal with certain aspects of your business but also do not want to hire employees. If you do not feel comfortable or competent in performing a necessary business task, whether it is weekly bookkeeping or laying a stone walkway, it is far better to find the right service to handle it than to neglect the job or botch it. Use your professional advisers — banker, accountant, and attorney — to help you find the services that will get your worst jobs done right. *Hiring employees will be discussed in more detail in Chapter 9.*

CASE STUDY: NETWORK, NETWORK, NETWORK

Nick Oliver, Managing Director
Euro Staff Solutions
Spain
www.eurostaffsolutionsonline.com

Nick Oliver started Euro Staff Solutions in April 2007 from his laptop to a turnover for 2008 of $120,000.

When working in different sectors and being involved with recruitment, I found the standards of interviews and recruitment procedures varied and poor. I had also used recruitment agencies and found most wanted to put bums on seats and collect their fees. I did not think this was good enough, and I wanted to create a company that focused on a personal service for both client and candidate. Meeting the client and candidate and talking to them, sometimes about the weather or sports events, gives our company a fantastic insight into the person or client.

Euro Staff Solutions provide the best staff we can for the vacant position on offer. We do not specialize in a particular sector because we have a wide knowledge base to work from. We have four staff members who work from home in a bedroom converted into an office. During the next 12 months, we potentially will move into offices to have a professional image and a smart base to work from. We use the Internet and e-mail as the main sources of communication at first and switch to telephone and personal meetings as projects progress. Because of our location, major projects during the summer months are temporary staff for the service industry, but we also place permanent staff in a variety of positions.

Having a staffing agency is hard work. There is fierce competition, so you have to be prepared to bend over backward for your clients and adapt to their needs. You will spend a large amount of time marketing in the beginning, but you do not have to spend fortunes. The golden rule is to network, network, network, so talk to everybody and anybody. Tell people about your company, and explain why it is so good. Tell them why they need your services. You are only as good as your last contract or client.

7

Legal Concerns

Now that you have had the opportunity to familiarize yourself with the different types of legal structures and some of the funding sources for launching and running your staffing service, it is time to start establishing and opening your business. You should start with the most basic step, which is to set up a temporary office so you have a home base to work on getting through all the other steps.

Set Up a Temporary Office

A temporary office is a location from which you can conduct all the preliminary research and get all the pieces together to open your staffing business. The preliminary work provides you with the information you need to select an appropriate name for your business and decide which business structure is the best one for you. The temporary office also allows you to get a better idea of the kind of location you will ultimately need to operate your business.

To do all this preliminary work, a home office works well. Start by setting aside room in your home for all the basic equipment you need and create enough space to spread out your research material. In addition, if you are establishing this operation with partners, you are going to want to have a setting available for private discussions other than the local coffee shop. *More about setting up a home office is discussed in Chapter 11.*

Items that you must have include:

- A desk with a comfortable chair
- A filing cabinet
- A printer, copier, scanner, and fax combination machine
- A telephone
- A laptop computer, which allows you the flexibility to take the information with you if you need to travel as you work
- Internet access

Having Internet access from day one is essential. Because there are still rural areas in the country where high-speed Internet is not available through a telephone service provider or cable network, investing in a USB broadband connection device is worth the expense. These devices are available through your cellular phone service provider and are billed as another phone line. Another alternative is to acquire service through a satellite receiver; however, there is a setup cost in addition to the monthly fees because the equipment that needs to be installed at your office can be costly.

If you initially set up your office at home, you should also install a separate business telephone line. It is more professional to have your business voice mail answer when you are not available than to have a family member take a message for you. First impressions, even through telephone contact, are critical. A business voice mail gives the caller a visual impression of a professional office, but a family member answering the line implies a small home office, which is often not perceived as professional.

Nothing is wrong with purchasing pre-owned office furniture and equipment because neither show wear often. Your purpose is to establish and operate a business that is financially successful. Spend your startup money wisely as you build your company.

Naming Your Business

When you are naming your staffing business, consider using words or terminology in the name that help people recognize what the business provides. Consider the names of some of the large staffing agencies in the industry. Aerotek Staffing Agency includes the term staffing agency to indicate it provides staffing services. The company named Manpower also implies staffing or employment services. Even if you decide to use your own name as the company name, you might want to consider adding a descriptor to the name for clarification. If you decide to name the company Jane Doe, a better option might be Jane Doe Personnel or Jane Doe Staffing Services.

The naming process takes place after you have determined the structure of the business you are proposing. You will want to be sure the name you select is legal and accurately reflects what your business does. Verify no other business in your area shares the name you are considering. You might have to file your name with your state or local government for approval.

Avoid long names that are hard to remember. You might brainstorm business name ideas with friends, business advisers, or others. Think of how the name will sound when you answer the phone and how it will look on a flier or other advertising. Reserve the URL or Web address of your website as soon as you choose a business name even if you do not plan to set the website up for a few months. Also, you might want to check the availability of selected Web addresses before you settle on a name.

If your business name is different from your real name, most states require you to file a fictitious name registration, DBA registration, or a similar form of registration to specify the name you are using to conduct business is not your own. The agency with which the fictitious name or DBA name is filed varies from state to state. In some states, the registration is with the city or county in which the company has its principal place of business. However, the majority requires the registration to be done with the secretary of state office. The only states that specifically do not require any type of filing when conducting business with a name other than your personal name are: Alabama, Arizona, Kansas, Mississippi, New Mexico, and South Carolina. Washington, D.C., makes it optional, and Tennessee does not require such filing for sole proprietorships or general partnerships.

Creating the Business Image

You can create an image for your business once you have determined your perfect company name — one that means something to you, makes you stand out, and sets you apart from the competition. Creating an image of how you want the general public, customers, and candidates to perceive your company is significant because people will identify with it and relate to what your company is about. Part of creating your image and developing it as your business grows is cultivating your company's professional attitude, culture, and business ethics.

An integral part of this image is your business logo. The logo must be different from anyone else's because the last thing you want is to have your company mistaken for another. Graphic artists, marketing agencies, and print shops are excellent places to go to for the design of your logo. Make sure to ask them for a high-resolution digital copy so you can reproduce it for all your business stationery and marketing needs. In addition to being able to find an abundance of graphic artists on the Internet, marketing agencies and local print shops always have graphic artists as part of their staff. You will also be able to find marketing agencies and printing companies on the Internet. However, tapping into your local talent by using local professionals is always a good idea, and your local phone book is the best source of information for that.

Obtain an Employer Identification Number (EIN)

All employers, partnerships, and corporations must have an employer identification number, also known as a federal tax identification number. You must obtain your EIN from the IRS before you conduct any business transactions or hire any employees. The IRS uses the EIN to identify the tax accounts of employers, certain sole proprietorships, corporations, and partnerships. The EIN is used on all tax forms and other licenses. To obtain one of these, fill out IRS Form 55-4, which you can find online **www.irs.gov/businesses/small**. Click on the link for small business forms and publications. There is no charge. If you are in a hurry to get your number, you can get an EIN assigned to you by telephone by calling 1-800-829-4933.

The IRS has developed a website called the Small Business Resource Guide, which has been specifically designed to better help small business owners and those who are just starting their business. This guide can be accessed online at **www.hud.gov/offices/osdbu/resource/guide.cfm**. Through this website, new business owners can access and download any number of the necessary forms and publications the IRS requires.

Permits and Licenses

Staffing businesses do not have any specialty licenses the owners are required to carry. Standard business licensing, however, does apply. Standard business licenses are those issued through city, county, and state licensing agencies.

City business license

You will almost certainly need a city business license if you are operating within a city, and you might need a county permit if you are not located within city boundaries. You can find out more about which licenses and permits you might need, where to get them, and how much they will cost by calling your city hall or county clerk's office. In most cities, the city clerk does not issue business licenses but can direct you to the correct office if you cannot find it on your own.

You need a city license for several reasons. You can be fined heavily for running a business without the correct permit. You also need to show your customers you are legitimate, and you will need a city business license in most states to get your sales tax permit. When you contact the agency that issues the city business license, ask how long the license is good for, what the renewal process is, what level you need if there are levels of licensing, how much it will cost, and whether you need anything else to be legal as a business within your city or county.

State and county permits and licenses

Depending on where you live, there might be state or county permits or licenses required to start a business. Call your secretary of state's office and your county clerk's office to make sure you are not missing anything you need to apply for.

How to know you have covered it all

The best way to make sure you have everything done is to ask someone who knows you. Small business organizations, such as SCORE and Small Business Development Consultants, are good resources for this. You might also want to call your local chamber of commerce and ask whether someone can help you make sure you have covered everything for your startup licensing and permits. Talking with someone doing business in your area can be a big help in making sure you are complying with all the relevant laws and regulations.

Once you have your business licenses and permits, it is time to consider the various types of insurance coverage your staffing business needs to carry.

CASE STUDY: NICHE TO BE RICH

Mary B. Harvey, APR, CPRC
Founder & CEO, Agency a la Carte
Subject Matter Staffers Inc.
Staffing and Recruiting for Advertising,
Marketing, and Public Relations
http://agencyalacarte.com
mary@agencyalacarte.com

I did not start out to run a staffing business. I started as a consultant in my field of advertising and public relations. Soon, I found my field lacked a coordinator for all the freelancers. Artists, writers, Web developers, and PR pros were all consulting on a freelance basis, but none liked to manage the process, budgets, contracts, and bills. So my firm began to handle that phase of their work. Eventually, it grew into a staffing and recruiting firm.

We do contract staffing, contract-to-hire, and direct hire recruiting in professional services of advertising, marketing, and public relations. We are specialized, and our recruiters are subject-matter experts. Here are my tips:

✓ Read *Free Agent Nation* by Daniel Pink.

✓ Hire an attorney with experience in staffing and recruiting.

✓ Hire a good CPA.

✓ Learn all you can about human resources.

✓ Learn all you can about cash management.

✓ Find the best software for recruiting and managing databases and assignments and get training.

✓ Join American Staffing Association and Staffing Industry Analysts. They are excellent resources.

✓ Read as much as possible about Generation X and Generation Y because you'll be hiring them and working with them.

✓ Take the Sandler Sales Training Program.

✓ Build a good website and optimize it as much as you can.

✓ Take full advantage of social media to drive people to your website.

8

Insurance

Insurance is a necessary expense, and in some jurisdictions, an absolute requirement for doing business. No matter how careful you are, accidents happen — insurance is your protection.

Types of Insurance

Insurance is not a one-size-fits-all solution. Laws vary by state, so some states will have higher premiums based on a number of factors, including the total number of claims filed. Many states have minimum business insurance standards. A description of some common types of insurance follows.

Comprehensive general liability insurance

Your state might require general liability insurance. Contact a business insurance agent in your area or the county clerk's office that issues business licenses to find out whether this type of insurance is required. This type of insurance covers your business against unexpected accidents and injuries. Review the policy for exclusions that might leave you vulnerable to exposure under certain circumstances. Do not ignore or skim the fine print.

Know the type of coverage you need and the type of coverage the insurance company is providing. Talk to a number of providers. Better yet, ask other business owners for referrals to reputable insurance brokers who deal with a range of insurance companies. An insurance broker will shop around for the coverage you need at the lowest cost. The most important part of this process is obtaining the proper coverage. A lower premium is not worth much if you find yourself without the insurance protection you need.

How much liability coverage is enough? A million sounds like a lot, but in today's world, that amount might not be enough. A good minimum is probably $2 million, and $3 million is even safer. If you can afford it, go higher. You will find insurance companies price this type of insurance reasonably if you do not have a history of claims and judgments, and premiums are not based on a dollar-for-dollar fee schedule. For example, $2 million in coverage is less than twice the cost of $1 million. An insurance broker who specializes in small business coverage can help you determine what you need. Be honest, and do not mislead him or her or yourself about what you will be doing in your business. Outline the types of staffing services you provide. Ask questions. Write down the coverage you need and the providor or broker's promises about coverage, and check these items against the actual insurance policy.

Bonding

If you already have general liability insurance, do you also need to have company and employees bonded? The answer is sometimes yes. Liability insurance covers accidental property damage or injury caused by you, the contractor, to your customer's property or people on the site, but it does not compensate for construction defects or poor workmanship. A surety bond is an agreement the contractor arranges with a bonding company to pay awards to the consumer if an arbitrator or legal action judges the contractor at fault when a job is not completed to the customer's satisfaction. State laws differ, but it is common for states to require contractors to carry surety bonds of a certain level depending on their license category. Bonding is a requirement for jobs with the government or large commercial jobs.

Although carrying both liability insurance and a surety bond is expensive, it helps attract and keep customers who understand their property and investment will be protected no matter what. Plus, you can then charge premium rates for your staffing services because not every staffing agency carries this coverage. You can find a bond provider who works with businesses in your state through the National Association of Surety Bond Producers at **http://www.nasbp.org/NASBP/NASBP/Directory/FindAProducer/Default.aspx**.

Employee bonding is a different matter. Employee dishonesty bonds are surety bonds that guarantee compensation if your employee steals property or is otherwise negligent on the job. You might want this coverage because, frankly, you never know what another person is thinking. Talk to your insurance agent to see whether it is necessary.

Workers' compensation insurance

Every state requires workers' comp, as it is commonly called. However, the structure of the insurance varies by state. Private insurance companies offer this coverage based on the number of employees on the payroll, the roles each individual performs, and the type of business you are operating. However, some states require such coverage to be obtained from the state government or one of its agencies. This insurance pays medical expenses and lost wages for workers who are injured on the job. There are exclusions for certain categories, such as independent contractors and volunteers, but check your state's laws. Business owners are exempt in most cases.

Home-based business insurance

Home-based insurance is required if you are working out of an office in your home. Homeowners' policies rarely cover business losses. If you are operating from your home or garage, check with your insurance agent to see whether anything in your office is covered. The typical homeowner's policy specifically excludes home-based business losses, including equipment damage, theft, loss of data, and personal injury. Unfortunately, many companies that provide homeowner's insurance do not offer business coverage, so you might need to have two insurance companies covering different areas of your home.

Criminal insurance

Criminal insurance covers you in the event of an employee committing a crime, which is in addition to bonding. General liability insurance might not cover theft or other criminal acts by employees. If someone is on your payroll, you might be held responsible for his or her actions while he or she is working with your customers. Should that person steal something, vandalize customer property, or deliberately harm someone, the customer will expect you to assume responsibility. This type of coverage can also protect you in the event of employee embezzlement. Depending on your general liability coverage, you might want to consider this category of insurance.

Surety bonds

Surety bonds are performance guarantees that fall under the insurance category. This is a way to assure a client or customer that your company will complete work as stated in a contract. Large commercial customers want to know you have the financial resources to get the work done. Surety bonds (also called performance bonds) are available from insurance companies. If you cannot get such coverage on the commercial market, the Small Business Administration has a surety bond program that might be available to you. As with all government programs, be prepared for paperwork.

Key man insurance

Lenders who provide capital for businesses might require key man insurance. This coverage applies to the person whose absence from the company would cause it to fail. Most likely, that person would be you or your partner. If you have borrowed money to start or operate your business, the lender might require such insurance as a guarantee of payment if anything were to happen to you.

Business interruption insurance

Business interruption insurance covers your expenses if you are shut down by fire, natural disaster, or other catastrophes. Some businesses are not as vulnerable to this as other types of businesses, so look carefully at your other coverage. Assuming your equipment and vehicles are already covered, you might not want to duplicate coverage. Discuss this with your provider or broker.

Insurance Review

Insurance is not an option — it is protection that is required by law and good sense. Business insurance has no single standard because laws, rates, and requirements vary by state. At a minimum, you will need comprehensive general liability insurance, workers' compensation insurance, and probably home-based business insurance. You might also consider product liability and criminal insurance policies. Your lender might require key man insurance if you have borrowed money for your business.

Ask other small business owners in your area for referrals to a reputable business insurance broker and review your options and requirements with her or him to determine the best coverage and find the best rates.

9

Hiring Employees

After your business is underway and you start going out to meet with the hiring managers of companies in the field, you might decide a voice mail message box or an answering service is not enough. Having someone in the office to answer the phones, call clients and candidates, do phone marketing, and schedule interviews and meetings for you has definite advantages. Some of this work cannot wait until after hours when all the other work is done. Some of this work needs to get done during normal business hours.

You might want to employ one or two office workers. Part-time help can be easy to find by asking friends or relatives if they know anyone with staffing experience or at least administrative experience. If you are reluctant to take a chance on a friend's recommendation, place a classified ad in your local paper, a local online publication, or a national site, such as Craigslist at **www.craigslist.org** or Monster at **www.monster.com**. You will probably receive more job applications than you can handle. *Software programs that help you manage applicant information are discussed in Chapter 10.*

Start the selection process before you place the ad by describing exactly what you want this employee to do, what experience he or she will need before starting, and which software programs or equipment skills the person will need to have. Your office helper might also become the face and voice of your business, so the person you choose should be able to get along with the public in person and especially on the phone. You might want someone who can also make cold calls to solicit business, and offer an extra bonus if an appointment is set. Instead, you might rather have a bookkeeper or someone to take over data entry responsibilities. Whatever it is you want, write it down, read it over several times, and picture the kind of person you feel suits the position. Personality counts in the staffing business.

Much of this same information applies to identifying and hiring candidates for your clients. The primary difference is that you will have to meet with the hiring manager for the company you are working with to gather all the information you need to find the candidate that fits their wants. *This will be discussed further in the second half of this chapter.*

Discriminatory practices

Under Title VII, the Americans with Disabilities Act, and the Age Discrimination in Employment Act, it is illegal to discriminate in any aspect of employment, including:

- Hiring and firing
- Compensating, assigning, or classifying employees
- Transfering, promoting, laying off, or recalling
- Advertising jobs
- Recruiting
- Testing

- Granting use of company facilities
- Offering training and apprenticeship programs
- Awarding fringe benefits
- Paying and giving retirement plans and disability leave
- Setting other terms and conditions of employment

Discriminatory practices under these laws also include:

- Harassment based on race, color, religion, sex, national origin, disability, or age.

- Retaliation against an individual for filing a charge of discrimination, participating in an investigation, or opposing discriminatory practices.

- Employment decisions based on stereotypes or assumptions about the abilities, traits, or performance of individuals of a certain sex, race, age, religion, or ethnic group or about individuals with disabilities.

- Denying employment opportunities to a person because of marriage to, or association with, an individual of a particular race, religion, or national origin or an individual with a disability. Title VII also prohibits discrimination because of participation in schools or places of worship associated with a particular racial, ethnic, or religious group.

According to laws the EEOC enforces, all employers are required to post notices detailing employee rights. These notices have to be reader-friendly for all people regardless of visual impairment or other reading disability.

All businesses, even small, startups like yours, should follow these guidelines. These are also laws and regulations that you need to be aware of when helping clients find the right candidates for their positions. Once you select a person to hire, you will need to set up a personnel file for him or her, prepare the appropriate government paperwork for tax withholding, and take care of other new-hire policies. If you are not sure what is required, your accountant, your state tax officer, or your local chamber of commerce can point you in the right direction.

You will also want to set aside time to train your new employee in the way you want the business to be handled. He or she might be spending a significant amount of time alone in the office if you are out at appointments and on sales calls trying to find new clients. You will want to closely monitor the results of the office work you assign to be sure the jobs are done. If there are problems, you will have to retrain or fire the individual. Neither of these tasks is fun; it is easier to pick your employee carefully from the start.

Finally, because you hired an office worker to take the burden off yourself, you will want to see increased revenue within a fairly short period of time. Be sure you do a cost analysis of your hiring experiment to see wheter it is bringing you more income or costing you more money than you expected.

Ideally, you will find someone who has knowledge of managing databases, managing telephones, and scheduling appointments. If you come across that kind of individual, find out why he or she is not employed. Experience alone is not a good indicator of a satisfactory employee. This person might have been fired because he or she was not dependable or competent. Successful business managers recommend zero tolerance for bad behavior, whether it is showing up late, exhibiting laziness, or constantly complaining without getting anything done. Make your policies clear from day one and put them in writing so there will be no misunderstandings if you fire someone at the job site.

It is not unusual for prospective employees looking for work to contact businesses. They might see one of your employment ads or come across your company from one of your other marketing efforts. Eager, experienced workers might drop into your lap, especially when the economy is not doing well. If times are good, you might have to be a little more proactive in your search.

Newspaper and Internet ads are effective at finding employees. Put together an ad that outlines exactly what you are looking for in someone to fill the position. Specify the work and hours, but consider whether you want to put the hourly pay in the ad. In some areas of the country, help wanted ads for staffing companies routinely contain the starting hourly wage. In others, a wage range is listed, and in other places, ads state that the hourly wages wil be competitive but do not list a specific number. Get to know the pay scales in your area for the work you want done, check the ads your competitors are placing, and use these standards as guidelines for creating your own ads. Also be sure to state in your ad that applicants must be currently eligible to work in the United States for any employer.

This is the only pre-screening you can legally do to make sure you are not hiring an ineligible worker. If you live in a large metropolitan area, you might get better results from community papers than from the large dailies that cover areas of 100 miles or larger. Online services, such as Craigslist (**www.craigslist.org**) and its local competitors, might be a cost-effective form of advertising. Just be sure your applicants are local. It is not wise to employ someone who lives two hours away and drives an old car that might not start on any given day.

Placing an ad that discriminates against anyone because of race, sex, age, religion, and other factors is illegal. You are looking for someone who can do the job no matter what other qualities the person might have or lack.

List your telephone number and e-mail address rather than an address or post office box number. If you do list your address and you are working out of your home, you might have unexpected visitors at your door at all hours. Using a post office box will delay response time, so it is not desirable for hiring in a rush.

Interviews

The interview process begins on the telephone as you are setting a time for a personal meeting with the candidate. The first thing to consider is the attitude of the person on the other end. Is he or she friendly or surly? Do not confuse an inability to articulate with a bad attitude. Someone might not have much formal education but have experience and a positive attitude that will overcome poor grammar. What is the demeanor of the person you are talking to on the telephone? Does this sound like a person you would like to be around? Some people might be shy about admitting they do not have experience or have other negative attributes. Lack of experience is not as big of a problem as someone who you suspect is being evasive or trying to pass off work experience at a fast food restaurant as the customer service experience you need to help you manage your staffing business.

Why does he or she want the job? Does he or she have an interest in the industry, or does he or she just need some money? Select the most suitable applicants before you schedule face to face meetings. You will want to know whether they have experience with the software programs and technological tools they will be using as your employee.

During the personal interview, apply the same standards you would expect your customers to use. How is this person presenting himself or herself? Is the person clean? Is his or her clothing torn or dirty? Does he or she look you in the eye during conversation? If the prospective employee claims to have experience, ask him or her two or three questions that require some knowledge to answer. You do not have to be challenging or harsh in your questioning. You can be friendly and even funny. You simply want to determine to the best of your ability whether this person is being honest with you. You might want to present a scenario and ask how the applicant would start, perform, and finish the task you describe.

Review the applicant's résumé and ask questions about gaps in work history or lack of recommendations from past employers. Someone who tries to turn that work history into a major qualification to work for you might not be as desirable as an employee. If you have the sense your candidate is lying, be cautious about hiring him or her. It is easier to not hire someone in the first place than to fire him or her after the fact.

Before you interview anyone, read the on rules on discrimination in hiring. Some questions are forbidden for you to ask during an interview. For example, you can not ask about a person's religion, politics, or sexual preference. Your questions should track the qualifications for the job, not outside interests or qualities the prospect has no control over.

It is not out of bounds to ask scenario questions during a job interview. Ask the interviewee what he or should would do if a candidate working on-site at a client's location calls the office upset about an incident that has occurred with the person they are working for at the company? Ask how he or she would calm the upset employee and handle contacting the person at the company that the employee is having a problem with. Discuss the job with the applicant and describe in detail what you would want that person to do. Check the person's reactions. If the candidate responds in a way that is completely unreasonable, smile, thank him for his time, and end the interview. Also avoid the applicant whose interview style is to present a list of demands he or she expects you to meet.

With each job applicant, try to objectively see the person. Is this someone you want to be around every day, someone a customer would like and trust, and someone you believe can help your company grow? all these things matter.

Hiring people you can promote is important because it gives employees reassurance they can grow along with your company and provides incentives for superior performance. Ambition can work for you. Do not be reluctant to hire the smartest people you can find.

Once you have narrowed your list and found the person or persons you would like to hire, check them out. Call former employers to inquire about their work histories and performance. Be aware that many former employers will be reluctant to offer bad news about someone. Know the qualities you want to inquire about, and ask specific questions. If you just ask a former employer what he or she can tell you about the candidate, you will probably get an answer as general as the question. You want to know whether the candidate showed up on time and did what he was supposed to do or caused problems. Listen for what the candidate's former employer is *not* telling you in addition to what he or she is telling you. If his former employer is distant or does not seem to have much to say about your candidate, this might be a warning sign. On the other hand, if he or she says, "I would hire him again in a minute," you have the answer you need.

Once you have made a decision, call the candidate and give him the good news. Tell him clearly, as you should have done during the interview, you have a probationary period of 60 or 90 days or another period you chose during which he can quit or you can let him go with no hard feelings and no obligation on either side. Send him a confirmation letter outlining your work policies and expectations. This can be a separate document. It is best to have all requirements and expectations in writing.

Contact everyone else you have interviewed and explain that you have made a decision to hire someone else. Wish everyone well and thank them all for their time.

Even after you select a candidate, keep the other résumés and contact information for people who seem appropriate. You never know when you might need another employee, and if someone who applied previously happens to be available, you will save yourself time finding your next hire. Even if you do not place them with your own business, you might be able to place them with a client that is looking for someone for a similar job position.

Some communities restrict how many employees a home-based business can have. Check your local zoning and other regulations before you commit to a number of people parking their cars and doing other business-related activities in the neighborhood. If you face such restrictions, you will be forced to rent business space or arrange for the employee to work from a remote location or virtual office.

New employee paperwork

No matter whom you hire, you will have to fill out and send in or retain certain government documents. These include W-4 forms, the Employee's Withholding Allowance Certificate, and the W-5 for employees with children if they qualify for advance payment of earned income credit. Check the IRS site or **http://business.gov/business-law/forms** to download forms.

Application of Federal Law to Employers

A number of factors might cause an employer to be covered by a federal employment law. These include the number of employees; the type of industry; and an employer's status as a private entity or a branch of federal, state, or local government.

The following chart shows how the number of workers a company employs determines whether a specific federal statute applies to the business:

Number of employees	Applicable statute
100	Worker Adjustment and Retraining Notification Act (WARN)
50	Family Medical Leave Act (FMLA)
20	Age Discrimination in Employment Act (ADEA)
20	Consolidated Omnibus Benefits Reconciliation Act (COBRA)
20	Older Workers Benefit Protection Act (OWBPA)
15	American with Disabilities Act (ADA)
15	Genetic Information Nondiscrimination Act (GINA)
15	Title VII of the Civil Rights Act of 1964
15	Pregnancy Discrimination Act (PDA)
1	Employee Polygraph Protection Act (EPPA)
1	Equal Pay Act (EPA)
1	Fair Credit Reporting Act (FCRA)
1	Fair Labor Standards Act (FLSA)
1	Immigration Reform and Control Act (IRCA)
1	Occupational Safety and Health Act (OSHA)
1	Personal Responsibility and Work Opportunity Reconciliation Act (PRWORA)
1	Uniform Services Employment and Reemployment Rights Act (USERRA)

Creating an Ethical Environment

In business, fraud refers to a deliberate action by an individual to cheat another individual or business entity. It involves some type of deceit for monetary gain at the expense of the other party. The most effective fraud deterrent is a corporate culture that does not tolerate fraud. Creating an ethical culture in the workplace is a process that takes time, investment, and continual education. To establish an ethical culture, both management and employees must be committed to it and willing to live by it every day.

Ethics policy or code of conduct

Every organization should have a formal ethics policy because it deters fraud and it legally supports efforts to enforce ethical conduct in the workplace. Employees who have read and signed a formal ethics policy cannot claim they were unaware their conduct was unacceptable. Recommended codes of conduct for various types of organizations are commercially available, but every organization should tailor its own ethics policy to suit its business and its needs. A good ethics policy is simple and easy to understand, addresses general conduct, and offers a few examples to explain how the code might be applied. It should not contain myriad rules to cover specific situations or threats, such as "violators will be prosecuted to the full extent of the law." In a legal trial of a fraud perpetrator, the judge, not the company, will decide the sentence. An ethics policy or code of conduct should cover:

- **General conduct at work:** Explain ethical and honest behavior is expected of all employees, and they are expected to act in the best interests of the company.

- **Conflicts of interest:** Employees might not understand what does and does not constitute a conflict of interest, so some simple examples are appropriate.

181

- **Confidentiality:** Make a company policy on the sharing of information among employees and departments or with people outside the company.

- **Relationships with candidates and customers:** Have a company policy on doing business with a relative, friend, or personal acquaintance.

- **Gifts:** Determine the types and amounts of gifts an employee might accept or give during the course of doing business.

- **Entertainment:** Describe the types of entertainment activities that are appropriate for vendors and customers and will be accepted on expense accounts.

- **Relationships with the media:** Make a company policy on who should communicate with the media about company affairs.

- **Use of the organization's assets for personal purposes:** This section should cover personal use of the Internet while at work and use of copy machines, telephones, and company vehicles.

- **Procedure for reporting unethical behavior:** Employees should be encouraged to report any large or small ethical violation. This section should explain how and to whom reports should be submitted and the use of a tip hotline if one exists.

- **Consequences of unethical behavior:** Discipline options should be clearly communicated and consistently enforced.

An ethics policy will not be effective if it is handed to each new employee and then forgotten. Ideally review the ethics policy with employees every year as part of an anti-fraud education program.

CASE STUDY: HIRING THE BEST PEOPLE

David and Philip Lowit
Principals and Co-Founders of
iSymmetry, Inc.
www.isymmetry.com

About iSymmetry

iSymmetry is a leading provider of on-demand consulting and recruiting services to global commercial enterprises and public sector clients. Founded in 1999, iSymmetry delivers high-end information technology and business management consultants. Areas of expertise include enterprise applications, customer relationship management, business intelligence, database design and development, business process management and software development.

About Philip Lowit

Philip Lowit is a principal and co-founder of iSymmetry. He is responsible for finance, business operations, consultant relations, and business capture. Before starting iSymmetry, he held positions at AT&T, Lucent Technologies, New York Life, and International Network Services. Philip brings more than 20 years of business leadership in the areas of financial management, sales, marketing, business strategy, and operations. He attended Rider University for a bachelor's in Accounting and Fordham University for an MBA. Philip is a CPA and is an active member of various industry and professional organizations.

After a successful run of working in corporate America, I had a desire to do something entrepreneurial. The staffing industry allowed us to leverage our business contacts, industry knowledge, and hard work into an excellent business.

About David Lowit

David is a principal and co-founder of iSymmetry. He is responsible for strategic planning, marketing, managing executive client relationships, strategic alliances, and driving new revenue opportunities. He possesses more than 20 years of sales and sales management experience in the technology services and communications industries. This includes structuring key supplier relationships in e-business, ERP, and CRM consulting environments at companies such as Accenture, IBM, and Deloitte. His background includes executive positions at GMAC, ATT, McCaw Cellular, and a number of startups. David is a CPA and holds a bachelor's in accounting from Rider University.

From a young age, I had an entrepreneurial itch to start a company. One of my interests is strategic corporate selling, and technology staffing was a way to leverage that strength.

Our staffing service is in the information technology staffing and management consulting field. We leave the readers with a few words of wisdom that helped us along the way.

Focus on creating a world-class organization, and always hire the best people you can find, even if it costs a little more. It's not enough to fill a client's requirements. A firm needs to consistently exceed hiring manager's expectations and create a reputation that keeps them coming back placement after placement, month after month, year after year.

Finding, Hiring, and Managing Candidates for Employers

The process for finding employees for your own office overlap with the process you use to find candidates for clients. The primary difference is you have to work with the client to get the information you need for finding the best candidates to present to the client.

The process works out similar to the following:

1. First, you receive client work order. The client contacts you, or you contact the client. The client determines a need to fill one or

more open positions. You will walk through a questionnaire with the hiring manager of the employer to get the specific details on the position.

2. Next, send your agreement to the client. The client agreement describes the role you will play in identifying, screening, and submitting candidates to the client. This agreement also includes the payment arrangements you discussed with the client up front.

3. Once the client receives, signs, and submits this agreement to you, you are ready to start looking for candidates who meet the client's needs and desires.

4. You can search for candidates in your own database or pool or seek new potential candidates by placing ads. Another way staffing services identify possible candidates is to contact individuals at other companies who are performing the same roles to ask for referrals. People in the profession tend to know others in the profession who might fill the needs you are seeking. The person you are contacting might even say he or she is interested in pursuing the job position for him or herself.

5. As you start to compile possible applicants, you will begin narrowing down your options by scheduling telephone or in-person interviews. Continue to narrow down candidates to those who are the top options. If the position requires background checks, reference checks, or any other criteria, handle it for the short list of candidates.

6. Present the top three candidates to the client for review and schedule interviews between the client and the candidates.

7. Depending on the outcome of the interviews, the client will either extend an offer to one or more of the individuals or tell you to keep looking.

8. If an offer is extended, contact the candidate, present him or her the offer.

If the offer is accepted, you remain involved as the liaison between the candidate and the client to schedule the start date and time. You even stay in contact with both parties up to the start date, on the start date, and for a period of time after the employee has been working there to ensure the relationship stays on track.

If the candidate is leaving his or her current employer, a counteroffer might occur when he or she gives notice. A counteroffer happens when a candidate accepts an employment offer from a client, but the current employer offers more money, benefits, or incentives to try to retain the employee and keep him or her from leaving. Be careful of this. If the current company's counteroffer is too good, you might lose your candidate for the open position.

If the candidate decides to accept the new permanent position, the candidate becomes the employee of the client. The client then takes over handling the new hire paperwork, which includes the job application, tax paperwork, and any other nondisclosure agreements or paperwork that the company requires of its employees.

If it is a temporary employee, the staffing agency keeps the job application of the candidate on file and has the candidate fill out a W-4 form for tax purposes. You should also obtain a copy of a government-issued photo ID, such as a driver's license, and a copy of a social security card, or the authorization for the employee to work in the U.S. All this information should be retained in the employee file.

CASE STUDY: THE DO'S AND DON'TS OF STAFFING

Justin Lipton, President
Environmental Recruiting Services
www.environmentalrecruiting.com
jlipton@environmentalrecruiting.com

Justin currently resides in Connecticut. He attended the University of Hartford, and shortly after graduation, he joined a major national staffing firm. As the IT industry was starting to grow, he joined a local firm and spent several years learning the sales and recruiting aspects of running a successful staffing services agency. After the company was acquired, Justin had a brief stint assisting with a startup company. From there, he founded Environmental Recruiting Services, a national search and recruitment firm targeting the environmental and industrial service industries.

I have been working in the staffing industry for about 20 years. I began my career working with a well-known, national firm. This opportunity was vital to my growth and the development of my skills in the industry. There is significant value derived from starting at the grass-roots level. It was there I learned the fundamentals of the staffing industry and the skills required for success.

I then accepted an opportunity within the IT industry just as it was beginning to thrive. There, I was exposed to and absorbed each facet of the industry. Later, a global firm purchased this firm. Unhappy with the new direction, I joined a former colleague and focused my efforts on the development of his new firm. I was responsible for all sales and recruiting efforts. This former colleague was not ethical, especially concerning our partnership. From that experience, I developed the confidence to go out and form my own company, Environmental Recruiting Services. Through my previous experiences with a variety of management styles and business models, I knew exactly how I would operate this business. The business model has proved to be a rewarding and fruitful endeavor.

I became a student of the business. I observed people who were successful and began to incorporate their techniques into the development of my own professional ideology. From that emerged an ability to facilitate cooperation on my terms. It is vitally important to establish terms that provide favorable outcomes for all parties involved. There is no harm in moving onto another client if the current client is not providing what is needed to produce favorable outcomes. When clients were receptive, I committed my time and energy to being available to them. Being unremittingly comprehensive from the beginning prevents most issues from developing later. I took the approach to work smarter and be thorough with each individual contact I made.

I knew I needed to be invested in every aspect to be truly successful in this business. Clients and candidates are working with me, not the company. Therefore, I always offered my undivided attention and was mindful of their needs while committing myself to understanding their goals. I recognized my hours would exceed the typical Monday-to-Friday, 9-to-5 p.m. work week to progress quickly in this business. I became engrossed in speaking with and learning from clients and candidates. I devoted as much time as was needed and viewed everyone I spoke with as a potential client or candidate.

Environmental Recruiting Services offers services nationally, so I communicate with businesses across various time zones. Early morning, late evening, and weekend hours are obligatory. Dedication is the foundation to a successful business in this industry and was an integral component in the establishment of mine.

My hope was to generate such volume that I could not handle the work without expansion. As the business grew, my goal was to hire individuals who were motivated and driven to succeed. Fortunately, I was able to accomplish that goal. I have the utmost gratitude for my staff. In sharing my vision and trusting in me, they have helped my business achieve its goals and continue to reach for more.

In addition to expansion, I strived for brand recognition. I wanted my company to be more easily identified nationally. Environmental Recruiting Services achieved this goal through the creation and implementation of an annual, industry-wide survey. Each year, we reach out to thousands of professionals across the United States and ask them to participate in providing industry-related data. The data encompasses industry demographics, compensation, work habits, concerns, interviews, and employment issues. This has proved to be a tremendous success and has helped us achieve our goal. The survey results have generated an influx of calls from new and existing clients requesting copies of the survey and our services.

I am looking to expand office locations, add service lines, revise the company website to offer more functionality, and offer comprehensive staffing services for the environmental and industrial service industry. These services include, but are not limited to, resume writing, career coaching, college recruiting, internships, and training.

I have achieved a true sense of accomplishment. There is something extraordinary about nurturing an idea from its inception and watching that idea grow into a profitable and successful business that, most importantly, involves the lives of others. I feel both proud and fortunate to work in a business that has the ability to establish and maintain long-term relationships with industry professionals. Working with people who have been laid off or are seeking a first job has taught me compassion, tolerance, and understanding. Working with candidates who travel so often it impedes time spent with family has taught me to recognize the diverse needs of each individual. I have had the opportunity to learn from people and the dynamics of their lives. I have affected their lives, and they have affected mine.

Good communication is paramount. The level of communication most often determines the level of service provided. When corresponding with clients and candidates, communication must be clear and concise from the beginning. This is important in establishing and understanding the goals and objectives of all parties involved. Additionally, when working with staff, an effective leader promotes communication in a way that creates an encouraging environment for personal and professional growth and development. The more motivated the individual, the more he or she will contribute to the company. Fostering open communication will better ensure consistent placement for both the client and the candidate while establishing predictability for staff.

Justin's Do's and Don'ts of the business:

Do: Establish a business plan with clear and concise goals.

Do: Set goals continually.

Do: Ensure staff members understand the goals and work collaboratively toward their achievement.

Do: Hold yourself responsible for the goals you set.

Do: Have an attorney with experience in the industry review your contracts. Also, have a knowledgeable accountant for consultation as needed.

Do: Thoroughly examine and select what is needed for your infrastructure, including e-mail, website, literature on your business, a business name, and applicant tracking software.

Do: Take copious notes and implement a tracking system to concisely notate important information. Do enter this data into the tracking system.

Do: Talk with everyone related to the industry. These people will provide valuable information for long-term success. Although there might not be a position for someone at that moment, something fruitful might present itself in the future for that person. By conducting a genuine conversation with someone, information about a qualified candidate or open positions might surface.

Do: Recognize your own strengths and weaknesses. Create opportunities to highlight your strengths and the strengths of others. Do hire someone whose strength is your weakness. If you are not strong with the accounting, advertising, or the IT side of the business, hire someone, even part-time, to help with those duties.

Do: Hire people who are passionate and competitive; however, ensure they will suit your corporate culture. These people will need to be aggressive and work diligently while collaborating well with existing staff.

Do: Believe in yourself. Your services are needed. Be confident when speaking with potential clients and candidates. You are a professional, and you know this business. Your candidates and clients will be looking to work with people who are confident and knowledgeable.

Do: Be prepared to hear no, and be ready to experience some struggles.

Do: Be tenacious; however, learn from your mistakes. Identify the things you can control and the things you cannot.

Do Not: Hire someone who will complicate things. Someone who comes in and disrupts the flow of the business will affect everyone negatively. Someone who complements the business is more likely to bring your company closer to its established goals.

Do Not: Be afraid to ask for help or advice from anyone. If you have a service that is of value, people will help you in any way possible and know you will assist them when it is time. Ask people to help you connect with a hiring manager or top candidates. Ask for advice from people who have more information or knowledge than you.

Do Not: Be afraid to walk away from business if the conditions are not optimal. If you have established a set fee and a client requests its reduction, decline unless an exclusive agreement is signed. You are working just as hard to fill that role as you will be to fill a role at full fee.

Do Not: Be afraid to relinquish some control to your employees. They will excel and grow professionally when given the freedom and flexibility to do so.

10

Money Management

If you have written your business plan, which includes your marketing plan, you know the clients you intend to target, which means you are also able to estimate where your income will come from. Where that income is allocated and how well it pays for your bills and operating costs is the focus of this section.

You need to look at your costs and what you expect to bring in each month and fill out a projected cash flow statement so you can see how your expenses are going to relate to your expected income. It is easy to get caught up in how much you will eventually be making, but inadequate cash flow has killed many businesses. It does not matter how much money you will make next month if you cannot pay the rent this month.

The Forms You Need

- **Projected cash flow statement:** This statement serves as a projection of cash coming in and going out each month for the first year in business.

- **Fixed costs estimate:** This estimate looks at the fixed expenses on a monthly basis, including rent, telephone, insurance, and fixed loan payments.

- **Variable costs estimate:** This estimate looks at the fluctuating monthly costs of doing business, such as office supplies, utilities, or office equipment maintenance or repair.

- **Income projection:** This projection addresses how much you expect to make in income.

- **Pricing structure worksheet:** This worksheet helps you calculate how much it costs per day for you to be in business and determine what beyond fixed expenses you need to build into your fees to make a profit.

You can find these sample worksheets in the sample business plan in Appendix A or in sample business plan templates you can find online.

Business success is directly connected to sound money management: keeping careful track of the amount of money that comes in, where it comes from, how much money goes out, and who receives it. Sound money management begins with knowing your costs. Ideally, you will calculate your best estimate of operating costs before you start your business. Build in regular re-evaluations to be sure your estimates are accurate once your business is underway.

You will want to know your basic cost of doing business, or the amount you need to meet just to remain solvent. If your monthly cost is $5,000, and there are 30 days in a month, you must make an average of $167 for each day of the month just to pay your basic expenses. You do not make any money until you exceed that amount. Start this process by estimating what it costs you to be in business for one month. Add up fixed costs, such as rent, phones, ongoing marketing expenses, and the costs of your office equipment spread out over their expected working life. Do not forget to add in the monthly costs of ink and paper. Account for other office equipment in the same manner to arrive at their monthly costs.

You will also need to figure in employee wages and benefits and many other costs. An accountant might be able to give you a more detailed approach to determine your costs. That is another benefit of working with a professional expert. The point is to have a realistic method of determining costs so you will know how to factor them into your pricing. Your cost of doing business should always be borne by the customer, not your business.

CASE STUDY: CASH FLOW TO SUCCESS

Karen Vandehei, Owner
Accurate Placement
P.O. Box 32324
Phoenix, AZ 85064
(602) 678-0144, ext. 14
www.accurateplacement.com

Accurate Placement is a staffing service that specializes in placing office staff in positions in various types of companies and in various industries. Positions range from entry-level clerical positions to mid-level management positions. When the company started in 1996, Karen Vandehei and her business partner chose to open and operate the company from a shared office space right away.

They opted for a shared space with an attorney they knew. Vandehei says sharing the space with the attorney was cost-effective because he did not charge them rent. Also, the location was perfect. However, nothing in business stays perfect for long, and when it comes to managing the income and expenses of the business, the obstacles are always there.

As with any business, Vandehei says there are cycles that can create cash flow issues. Because Vandehei and her partner funded Accurate Placement, they always watched the upcoming payroll to make sure they had enough cash on hand to cover it. For example, Vandehei says if the company receives a job order from a client for which they place numerous temps in the positions, she needs to have enough cash available to cover the payroll for the temps for 30 to 60 days, and in some cases up to 90 days, before receiving payment from the client.

Vandehei says Accurate Placement opts for alternative financing, which is available with companies that factor invoices. Companies buy outstanding invoices from other companies, which is called factoring invoices, so the company selling the invoices has cash flow until the client with the outstanding invoice pays it. It is similar to using an invoice as collateral for a loan. This is how Accurate Placement funded the payroll in the early days and until the company had enough money to carry the business and cover the payroll on its own.

Taxes

Taxes are a critical factor in sound money management. It is essential to maintain records of all sales and expenses down to the last penny. The IRS will want to see what came in and what went out, especially if your business is ever audited. Clear, up-to-date records show you are a responsible taxpayer and help avoid any suspicion of shady policies. Keep your company above board and financially transparent to the parties that have a legal right to see the numbers.

You are not keeping accurate books as a favor to the government. Your financial records are an ongoing map of your business's life. If you do not keep accurate and detailed numbers, you will not have any idea how your company is doing financially. You must have the numbers and be able to understand them to know whether you are meeting your goals and have a decent profit margin.

You will want to make sure your federal, state, and local taxes are filed in time. In some places, you might be required to collect sales tax on services and periodically pay it to the governing body. Verify these requirements by contacting your city or state tax department. They will tell you which licenses or tax filings are necessary and the schedule and appropriate ways to file. Many taxing entities are converting to online tax filings for businesses. You will need to set up a special account on the related government website to use online filing and payment methods.

Controlling Costs

Controlling costs is the most challenging aspect of business. You are not in business as entertainment or just to occupy your time. You are in business to make money. You must accomplish two things: find customers who will pay you fairly for your services, and control your business spending to enable you to make a profit. Many small businesses, especially new ones, find their cash flow is out of control and, even though accounts receivable is healthy, they do not have the money on hand to pay bills or payroll on time. This is where budgeting and cost controls become critical.

Your company's cost controls begin when you pay for your first item whether it is to install your business phone line or to buy a box of paper clips. It is to your advantage to shop around, determine the going rate for your target purchase, and look for discounts on that rate. A small accounting firm that specializes in small businesses might offer lower rates than a large firm that must cover the overhead costs of a fancier office and numerous employees. You might also find the service is more personal when dealing with a small law firm or accounting practice.

Never blindly accept any price. Ask yourself how any product or service can be obtained for less money. You might not get as low of a price as a chain store or big business, but you do have the ability to move to lower cost suppliers who will deliver the quality you expect. As you put together your monthly, quarterly, and annual budgets and cost estimates, plan to spend as little as possible. When you start out in business, it is wise to stick to the basics and save the luxuries for a later day. It might be tempting to be a bit extravagant here and there and buy a nice leather chair for your office or a fancier desk, but you cannot make money if you are spending it all. Develop a frugal mindset.

Breakdown of Costs

One of the best ways to manage the costs and expenses of the business is to review and understand the breakdown of the cost you will have. The costs might fluctuate depending on whether you choose to run the staffing service at home or from a rented space and whether you choose to run it solo or hire employees to help you with the work.

Utilities

With utility deregulation underway in some states, you might be able to negotiate your gas or electric rate by considering alternate suppliers. In the past, a business had to be large or use vast amounts of energy to bargain for better rates. That is not always true now. Some states even offer alternative energy suppliers for residential customers or allow you to choose utility providers other than the one servicing your area. It simply means switching to another provider that offers you the same services at a less expensive rate.

There are also numerous ways to reduce your consumption of gas and electricity. It might seem inconsequential to save pennies on your electric bill, but if you start there and force similar savings on everything you do, the pennies will add up in the long run.

Low-energy light bulbs are good for the environment and use less electricity. There are many brands and options. Take advantage of them. If you have gas heat, make sure the system is working efficiently and has a clean filter. If you are working out of your home and are taking a tax deduction for your office space, be aware that basic cost efficiencies in your home will eventually translate into dollars for you. Take your utility company's advice and perform an energy audit of your home and office. Water should not be a major expense at your office or your home.

Office expenses

The office is a good place to control costs. Developing systems and strategies that keep your operating costs down even a few cents at a time will add up in the long run.

Control the costs of your stationary, for example. A professional-looking letterhead with a single color will suffice. Envelopes, business cards, order forms, contracts, and other forms can look crisp and professional at a low cost. You can print some forms yourself. You might buy office supplies online through a discount supplier or from an office supply warehouse. Buy in bulk if you will use a large amount of the product, but avoid oversupply, especially if you have limited storage in your office.

If you lease equipment for such services as credit card processing and postage, shop around for the best deal. Practice your negotiating skills on every product and with all vendors even when your target product or service is advertised on sale. You might be shocked by the price variations for the same service with the same piece of equipment. Every vendor you deal with has the same goals you have for your business: gaining the highest possible profit margins. Beware of unnecessary upgrades a company might try to sell, and keep your basic goal of quality in mind while covering the essentials.

Controlling loan costs

If you borrowed money to go into business or arranged for a line of credit to purchase equipment or smooth your cash flow, you must budget to make repayments. Seek the lowest interest rates and the best terms for the money. Fees, closing costs, and document processing can raise the cost of borrowing money, so apply the same standards here as you would apply to vendors. If your credit is good, you will discover most lenders are happy to deal with you and are willing to negotiate. If your credit is not as good, it might mean higher interest rates, increased fees, and special charges. Do your best to improve your credit score by borrowing as little as possible and paying on time and in full. If you maintain good financial habits, your credit score eventually will rise and the cost of borrowing money will go down.

Controlling marketing costs

Marketing is essential to your business's well-being, but it can also be a budget buster. Your annual marketing plan might include placing an ad in the telephone book's yellow pages and similar publications. Avoid the temptation to go for a full-page advertisement despite what a salesperson might tell you about its benefits. You will want a yellow pages presence, but you do not need to spend big dollars. There can be a significant lag time for such annual ads. If your business is like most startups, you will have a limited marketing budget. It is advisable to spread it around to get the best value. The only worthwhile marketing is what makes you money. For example, many businesses are relying heavily on social media marketing as part of their business marketing plans. Social media marketing can create exposure and publicity for your staffing business and is free after the cost of time it takes to manage your social media accounts, such as Twitter, LinkedIn, and Facebook. *You can learn more about marketing and advertising options in Chapter 12.*

Dues

Your membership in organizations such as the chamber of commerce, Business Networking International (BNI), and local or national professional groups will bring you business, so budget money to pay your dues. Plan to spend several hundred dollars per year for these memberships plus whichever application or initiation fees are involved. Most of these groups will have some period during the year in which they waive these fees as initiatives to increase membership.

If you find the cost of membership in all the groups you identify will not fit in your initial budget, determine the one or two of these organizations that will be the most beneficial. Talk to other professionals about the groups they have joined, and ask them which provide the most leads or customers. In some cases, BNI produces more residential business than the local Chamber of Commerce, but the Chamber ultimately can offer business-to-business contacts that you might otherwise miss.

Memberships in business groups have one unavoidable fact: You must show up and be active or you will be wasting your money. Membership alone does not bring in business. You must go to the meetings, pass out your business cards, work a booth at the annual fundraising picnic, volunteer for whichever charity your group supports, and help other members increase their businesses just as you are asking them to help yours.

One way to do this is to discuss with other business owners or managers the biggest hiring or employee challenges they are facing with their business right now. By listening to what their responses are, you can pick up clues as to what services you have to offer that can help them overcome these challenges. When you are discussing the position each person holds at their company, try to determine if he or she is in a hiring position or if he or she is able to put you in touch with one of the people in charge of hiring for the company.

Employees

If you choose to hire a full- or part-time employee to help you in your staffing business, be aware the cost can be far higher than you anticipate. You have two choices to get work done: Hire someone whose taxes are deducted by your company, or sign up someone who is an independent contractor for whom you would file a 1099 income tax form. A person working under a 1099 uses a federal tax ID or Social Security number and operates his or her own business. This type of worker is responsible for his or her own taxes. Individuals who provide their services to a number of small businesses prefer this arrangement. You might find yourself using this type of worker if all you need is occasional help. You will not be expected to pay benefits or Social Security deposits for this person, but you must be careful not to refer to independent contractors as employees or demand they work specified hours, at specified locations, or be under your control. The IRS is aware businesses might attempt to use contractors to avoid paying payroll taxes. You want to be sure you do not violate the rules for 1099 work. Ask your accountant for an opinion.

An independent contractor is required to choose his or her own times to work. A potential independent contractor will likely choose to work the hours you would prefer, but if the contractor wants to take a two-hour lunch break, you are not permitted to punish him or her if the work is done on schedule. If the worker is under your control, he or she is working as an employee, not a contractor. If you use an independent contractor, you have the right to control or direct only the outcome of the work, not the techniques or processes performed to achieve the result.

People who work as independent contractors generally charge more per hour than what you would pay an employee because they must pay their entire FICA tax and many of their own expenses, including marketing costs. Independent contractors generally work for several different firms and juggle their hours during the week to accommodate several clients. The contractor decides whom to work for and when, not the businesses who request his or her services.

If you use an independent contractor, you will submit at tax time an IRS-approved 1099 form to the contractor and a separate copy directly to the IRS that shows the total compensation the person received from you in the previous year. This is done, in part, to keep the contractor honest. Independent contractors are responsible for reporting all earnings by filing a Schedule C to deduct expenses like any other business and paying all required taxes.

If you hire a full-time employee, expenses for wages and insurance shift to you. In addition to base pay, employers pay all the other costs associated with maintaining an employee, including workers' compensation insurance, unemployment benefits, and the Social Security tax for each employee. Half is the employer's responsibility, the other half is deducted from the employee's gross pay. Additional costs might amount to 24 percent or more over base pay. The IRS employer tax information is available in hard copy or online at **www.irs.gov/publications/p15/ar02.html**.

A full-time employee could easily cost your business more than $40,000 per year. You also have to follow labor department guidelines for overtime and other employee labor rules that are not relevant to contractors. Having one or more full-time employees on your staff means you are writing paychecks every month, even when business is slow. How much business do you need to justify that kind of expense? It is a basic business assumption that employees *make* money for their employers, so you will have to do the math to make this work for you. You must make enough to pay for employee salaries and a little more to pay for marketing, insurance, and all the other costs of doing business before you break even. It is easier to add benefits than to take them away, so be cautious as you go through the hiring process. Your first responsibility is to your business. It is not good for anyone if you are forced to let someone go because you do not have the financial resources to honor your employment package.

If you only need part-time help, you might choose to hire part-time workers for your busy season. Unlike independent contractors, part-time employees are under your control. Although you are required by the government to pay taxes on the amount they earn, just as if they were full-time employees, you might not be required to provide certain other benefits that are obligations for full-time help. Check with your accountant and the IRS if you are unsure of your financial responsibilities.

Cost of business

As mentioned above, it takes money just to keep the doors open for business. There will be expenses to pay regardless of whether you have customers. You have business cards you will need to replace because you are passing them out to everyone you meet. There are also the costs of contracts, invoices, and letterhead. Some of your office equipment will break and need to be replaced. You will need to replace paper.

There is no getting around the need for tight budgeting of the everyday costs you will incur. Major equipment purchases are one-time expenses, and you can spread their costs over time as you work with your accountant to categorize major expenditures. Examine each category, and be tough in your budgeting. Look for ways to save money, and confine your spending to what your business needs, not what you want.

Special expenses

Not every expense can be foreseen. Your biggest client could be 60 days late paying its invoice. If you do not have enough cash in reserve, this might mean you do not have money to pay office rent, the electric bill, or even your payroll. Some items are difficult, if not impossible, to budget in advance. You can, however, apply your normal conservative budgeting philosophy to special projects or other unusual circumstances. One such circumstance would be a large project for which you are taking on a subcontractor. In this case, you have two requirements for prospective subcontractors: First, are they competent enough to do a good job? Second, is their price fair and can you mark it up and still provide the customer with a project cost that is competitive?

As you budget this project, consider your subcontractor's qualifications and who will be responsible for cost overruns, project upgrades, and other changes. This is another example of the need for detailed contracts that outline all responsibilities and thorough research of your potential partners in any project. If you are the primary contractor, the customer will turn to you to resolve problems. If your subcontractors have problems getting the job completed in a satisfactory manner, your customer will look for solutions from you, not to the subcontractor who did a poor job.

Problems will arise. It is a natural part of business. If you plan to be in business for a long time, you must work hard to develop a reputation as a solid business. You can only do that by building a list of satisfied customers who are eager to refer you to their friends and colleagues. Angry or disappointed customers will drag your business down.

Responsible budget management might mean short-term sacrifices for long-term gain. Avoid the temptation of cutting corners to achieve short-term satisfaction. You are in this for the long run, so keep your expenses lean while acknowledging every day as an investment in your future and the health of your business.

Setting financial targets

While you are still in the planning stages of opening your business, take the time to lay out an initial budget and make preliminary income forecasts with your banker and accountant. Set a particular target income for the first three years at a minimum. Then, work backward to figure out how many companies you will need as clients to reach that income level and what you will do to find those customers. Taking a hard look at your income potential before you start will place you in a realistic position from the beginning so you will build and maintain a profitable business.

When it comes to the staffing industry, average small business operations can bring in as much as $750,000 annually. Other small business firms reach $15 million. The figures for your own business can vary wildly depending on your niche, geographic area, and spending practices.

Evaluating your progress

Even though you set targets and think you know where the money will be coming from, circumstances change. By re-evaluating your business monthly or quarterly at first and then going to an annual evaluation, you will focus on what you are doing and where you are heading and can make the necessary course corrections. Once again, enlist your accountant in this process. He or she might be able to show you how to compare reports on your software accounting program that will give you the detail you need.

11

Organization of the Office

More than half of America's small businesses are home-based, according to the Small Business Administration. A home office might be ideal for your business if you have space for it and your community allows home-based businesses. Before you decide a home-based business is right for your staffing service, you should first examine the zoning issue. Many communities have restrictions on businesses based in private homes mostly because of the traffic and other issues associated with operating a business. Check your local zoning laws by contacting the county or city zoning board, which you can find with a Web search or in the local phonebook. Explain the type of staffing service you intend to open. You might be required to pay a license fee.

Assuming it is legal for you to base your business at home, why would you want to?

First, the commute is great. You do not have to pay rent, and there can be some tax benefits. The IRS has strict guidelines for claiming a home office as a business expense, so discuss the details with your accountant.

Can You Succeed Working Out of Your Home?

Not everyone can afford an office space, and not everyone needs one. Executive recruiters who recruit from all over the country or all over the world might not need an office because they are not meeting with candidates in person. It is often possible to succeed with a home-based staffing service, but you should consider what you need and how you can make it work.

- **Can you create the space you need?** Most people find they can repurpose a guest room or remodel a garage to build their office space.

- **Can you work on location?** If you work mostly outside your home, you might get away with a computer on the dining room table for a while. Most people who do not meet with candidates do a large percentage of their work by phone or by meeting company clients at their work location.

- **Will there be a good working environment?** If you have small children at home and you absolutely cannot afford an outside office, you will have to work at home with your small children. But if the home environment makes work difficult and you can afford outside space, it is probably worth the cost to rent an outside office or studio.

- **Are you disciplined enough to work from home?** This is one of the first questions many people ask when they consider working out of their homes. The fact is, some people simply cannot get past the distractions of home and need an office outside the house to get their work done. They must separate their home lives from their professional ones.

Setting Up Your Office

If you are planning to operate your business from home, you will need cooperation. Explain to your family you are going to need to reserve a room, and then plan your workspace. Make sure it is large enough to be comfortable and efficient for everything you will do there, including contacting clients and candidates and the day-to-day aspects of marketing, scheduling, and payroll. A tiny desk in a corner might not work. You will need space for a large desk, filing cabinets, a computer, a printer, possibly a meeting table, at least two chairs, and an area to spread out résumés and client files. You might want to set up an extra place for an assistant to answer the phones or do bookkeeping when you are out.

Choose a quiet spot. You cannot work well if children are yelling, trains are going by, dogs are barking, and a television is on in the background. You will not present a professional appearance if a customer has to ask, "What's that noise?" You will not be giving your business the attention and focus it needs if you are distracted.

Phone

If you want to be listed in the yellow pages, you will need to have a phone dedicated to business. Some people only use a cell phone, but the dedicated land line is preferable. You also will need a fax machine and possibly a dedicated fax line, which can double as a second business line for calls if necessary. Rather than installing a separate line, you can opt to use an e-fax service so your fax line is a number that sends faxes directly to your e-mail. If you choose to use your cell phone as your primary business number, you might regret it when your phone rings constantly at job sites. A voice mail on an office line can be accessed remotely, so you will always be able to check your messages from job sites.

A two-line business phone is not a luxury. Line one is designated as the primary business line. Line two can be assigned as the fax line and also used to make outgoing calls. Some phone companies offer distinctive rings for faxes coming in so you do not pick up the phone. Telephone prices vary according to quality and features. Find the best one you can afford. Consider models with caller ID and automatic dialing. If you do not plan to use an answering service, consider a telephone service that offers voice mail. The device will tell you when callers left messages, so you can prioritize your call returns. You can save yourself some neck discomfort from frequent calls by getting a headset.

Fax machine, copier, and scanner

Many small businesses use all-in-one machines for faxing, copying, and scanning. The prices are reasonable, and they work well. The more expensive models have extra features and might be more durable. These are inkjet printers, not laser machines, which cost significantly more money.

Calculator

You will need at least two calculators. Your office should have a desktop calculator. They are easier to use, have larger number pads, provide printouts of your calculations, and have features for working up client proposals, such as the markup on the candidate's salary or hourly wages for determining your fee. The second calculator can be a small pocket model, cell phone, or PDA that you will use in the field for quick bids, balances, and other calculating needs.

Postage meter

This is an optional piece of equipment that you lease. How much surface mailing will you do? If you are just going to send out a few pieces of mail every month to pay bills or send letters and invoices to clients, you might not need one. If you are going to send out mass mailings to potential customers as part of your marketing strategy, a postage machine might be a wise choice. You are likely to overpay if you guess on postage for anything larger than a letter. A scale and meter combination will give you an exact postage amount and can print out a stamp just like the post office. Meters pay off only if you mail enough to offset the cost of leasing the machine, which varies according to features.

You can also order postage online from the U.S. Postal Service **www.usps.com** or download postage from their website to your computer through the new online postage services described here: **https://www.usps.com/business/online-postage.htm**.

Office supplies

Standard office supplies include letterheads, envelopes, business cards, and printer ink cartridges. You want a professional letterhead that features your company's name, telephone number, fax number, and your address. If you are working out of your home and do not feel comfortable revealing this to customers, you might prefer to use a post office box for your business mail. You will want a return address where people can safely send payments. If you want a logo or something other than basic type, you might wish to have a graphic designer create something simple, professional, and easy to read. You can also choose a tasteful example from a quick-printer's sample book. There are templates in most word processing programs you can adapt. This method allows you to print a basic letterhead on your own computer.

Envelopes should reflect your letterhead in style and tone. Use No. 10 business-sized envelopes. If you decide to include a return envelope, it should be a No. 9 to fit inside with your statement.

A No. 10 envelope will accept standard letterhead folded horizontally in thirds. There are two types: window and closed envelopes. Businesses frequently use window envelopes because the mailing address of the intended party on the inside form shows through the envelope's window. Closed envelopes require the address of the recipient either be printed on the envelope or on a sticker. If you decide not to have envelopes printed and do not want to run them through your computer printer, you can either print labels with your return address or purchase a rubber stamp. When you buy rubber stamps, consider getting one imprinted with "For Deposit Only" and your bank account number to protect checks from being forged if they are inadvertently lost or stolen before you take them to the bank.

Business cards are essential. You will pass them around to virtually everyone you meet; potential customers are everywhere. Business cards should be easy to read. There is nothing more irritating than staring at a business card that has so much information you cannot find the number to call or the service being offered. The card should state your company's name, your name and title, a primary phone number, fax number, e-mail address, and possibly your cell number. The card is already busy with just the basics. A simple logo or none at all is fine. Get the cards printed to give them a professional appearance. You can go to one of the office supply or chain printers for cards, letterhead, and other such items at a reasonable cost. You also might find companies on the Internet, such as Vistaprint (**www.vistaprint.com**) and 48HourPrint.com (**www.48hourprint.com**), which will offer quick turnaround at low prices for such products.

You might also want pre-printed invoices, estimate sheets, and service lists. It is acceptable to print these on your computer as long as they look professional.

Computers and Software

PCs and Apple° Macintosh computers and their variants are both fine for your business. Macs might be less virus-prone and are considered reliable, but they are also more expensive and have fewer specialty business software programs designed to work with them because there are fewer Macs in most businesses. PCs are often less expensive and have thousands of software programs available and more brands to choose from, so you can shop around. The price of PCs has come down so much it would be hard to justify purchasing a used one. Some new PCs are in the $500 range with a monitor included. Whichever you buy will probably be out of date in a couple of years.

Your first consideration is what you need to make your business run. You are going to access the Internet, probably with a cable, wireless, or DSL broadband connection, so you will need speed and power for that. Most likely, you will be keeping your books on the computer, processing job orders, maintaining files, creating spreadsheets, faxing, storing, and printing. Use software programs that help with tasks specifically related to your business.

Database or employee and applicant tracking software programs include:

- Complete Office Automation for Temporary and Staffing Services (COATS)
- MAESTRO Staffing Management System

- TempWorks Payroll

Each of these programs acts a depository for applicant and employee information. You can upload and edit résumés. These software programs also allow you to track work history, work interests, and other characteristics. Maintaining your résumés and applicant information in these databases makes the search process much easier when you are looking for a candidate with specific experience or work history with a particular client.

Receivables software programs include:

- eEmpACT
- MAESTRO Staffing Management System
- TempWorks

The receivables software programs permit you to effectively and efficiently manage your back office. These programs allow you to create payroll checks, invoices, letters, and client statements. In addition, you can use these programs to calculate deductions, update invoices, and update client accounts.

Recruiting software programs for staffing services include:

- eEmpACT
- myTTraz

Recruiting software helps you to identify and keep track of candidates from various sources, including the Internet.

Testing software programs help evaluate candidates and their skill sets, such as:

- Prove It!

- Qwiz
- SkillCheck
- Pre-Valuate

Explain your needs to the computer companies or retailers you are dealing with and compare their responses. If you have friends or family members who are more computer savvy than you are, ask them for their advice.

Desktop or laptop?

Both options have benefits and drawbacks. The desktop computer probably will have a bigger screen and an easy-to-use keyboard, and your printer, modem, and other external devices are plugged in. A desktop might cost less than a laptop, but you cannot take it into the field to use for presentations and proposals. A laptop is portable, but it costs more. The cheapest route is to select the most powerful desktop you can afford to get the most computing power for your money. You can purchase a laptop when your business has grown and you have more cash to spend.

You might want to purchase an external hard drive to back up or archive your document files and other essential records at least once a week to avoid data catastrophes. Back up or copy in an archive all important data, such as contact information, invoices, and your financial records, at least once a day or every time you work on a file. You might also want to consider an online backup system in addition to your external hard drive. Two reasonably priced options are offered by Mozy (**http://mozy.com**) and IBackup (**www.ibackup.com**). Regular backups protect your data from electrical blackouts, viruses, and other calamities.

Business software

Most new computers do not come automatically loaded with the software necessary to operate whether it is a PC or Mac. Verify this when you are negotiating the purchase to ensure you have access to a word processing program, Internet browser, an e-mail program, and other programs you need to run your business. You can consider Microsoft® Office, an office suite that includes Word, Excel, PowerPoint®, and Internet Explorer. You can purchase a similar system for a Mac, the Pages software, but Macs also work well with Microsoft® products. There are many other word processing programs, some of which are free. Check Open Office at **www.openoffice.com** for samples. At this time, most businesses use Microsoft, so if you want to easily transfer files to other companies for bids and proposals, you can assume they want them in Word. Beware of word processing or other programs with limited functionality.

Computer security

Firewalls and anti-virus programs are essential tools in computer protection. European Union computer security experts estimated in 2007 that viruses begin to attack new computers on the Internet within seconds. Firewalls, whether hardware, software, or a combination of the two, protect your computer from unwelcome intrusions.

Virus protection programs protect your computer against specific, known viruses. Symantec™ (**www.symantec.com**), McAfee® (**www.mcafee.com**), and Norton™ (**http://us.norton.com/antivirus**) are among the best-known software providers of this type of protection. Their programs must be updated regularly — preferably every day — to guard against the latest viruses, so you will want a renewable subscription, which is less than $100 annually for the basics.

Be conscious of spammers, who send out millions of e-mail messages for products or services you have never requested, and the phishing schemes they pursue. A phishing scheme is when a fraudulent e-mail or website is created that looks exactly like a real company's website or e-mails. The e-mail or website, however, is created to collect your personal or business information in an attempt to steal money, open new accounts, and otherwise steal your identity. The simplest way to protect yourself is to never click a link sent by someone you do not know, especially if the person claims to be a webmaster at a bank, your Internet service provider, or some other source that sounds legitimate. If you are doubtful, phone the company that is supposedly requesting the information from you. You want to make sure you have every resource available to protect your computer against the latest schemes of hackers who want to access your bank accounts, credit cards, passwords, and all the other information you need to protect.

Accounting software

There are numerous brands of accounting software. Some are so popular other software providers create add-ons that improve the functionality of the software. Work with your accountant to coordinate bookkeeping efforts.

QuickBooks™ is one of the most widely used programs. It is offered in both PC and Mac versions. There are small business versions that allow you to balance your checkbook, do your payroll, track expenses by category, and create custom forms. You will want to discuss all the accounting details of your business with your accountant before you set up your books so you will all be on the same page. You might not understand many of the accounting terms he or she uses, such as accrual or cash basis. QuickBooks™ takes a little practice to use effectively, but it is not difficult if you take an hour or two to get the basics, set up accounts, and gain some understanding of what it does. QuickBooks offers a contractor edition of its software that allows you to track job costs and profits and manage progress on several jobs at once, which is useful for a staffing service that has different clients. This is especially true if you place more than one candidate with a particular client or have a high volume of work with the company.

However, QuickBooks (**http://quickbooks.intuit.com**) is not the only highly rated business accounting program available. Sage Peachtree (**www.peachtree.com**), MYOB Business Essentials™, NetSuite® Small Business Accounting (**www.netsuite.com**), and Sage Simply Accounting™ Pro (**www.simplyaccounting.com**) are others. They will all provide the basic features you need to run your business, and they offer special features besides helping to balance your checkbook and calculate payroll taxes. They offer sophisticated business applications that can help you grow your business.

Once you have a good accounting program and have categories set up correctly, you will not need your accountant every day. Instead, your accountant can do weekly, monthly, or even quarterly oversight and monitoring. If you do not enjoy working with the figures, you might choose to hire a part-time bookkeeper to maintain the numbers and perform data entry. However, if you hire someone else to oversee your financial resources, check the records periodically to be sure everything adds up, or ask your accountant to review your employee's work if you do not understand it. Companies of every size have had to grapple with misuse of funds or embezzlement. The best way to prevent this is to keep monitoring the books or have someone you trust do it for you.

You will want to start your business financial dealings by using a separate business bank account. It is confusing and risky to mingle your personal funds with the business resources. Maintain a business checking account under the business name. Deposit all business checks into that account. Even if you are funding the business with your own person savings, write a check into the business account so it becomes a business contribution and business assets. Have credit card payments deposited there. If a customer pays you cash, deposit the money into the business account. If you are operating as a sole proprietorship and need to pay yourself for the work you have performed, write a check from the business account to yourself, then deposit it into your personal account. Run your business squeaky clean to avoid nasty problems tomorrow. The following are some basic accounting terms you might want to discuss with your accountant. Together you can decide what will work best for your particular situation.

Cash versus accrual. The cash method is recording a sale when the money is received and an expense when the cash goes out. This measures only what happens in your business, not necessarily when you made the sale. Accrual is recording the income when you invoice the job and recording expenses when they are incurred, not when they are paid.

Double entry versus single entry. Double means every one of your business entries is registered twice: once as a debit, once as a credit. You must be sure everything balances. Dollars are recorded coming in and going out. Single-entry bookkeeping is easier but is more prone to mistakes because there is no automatic balance. Your accountant will probably use the double-entry system.

Debit versus credit. Debit is the payout. Credit is when you got the money. Your company buys a rake. The rake is a debit. The money to pay for the rake is the credit.

Calendar year versus fiscal year. Businesses operate on a 12-month cycle. Theoretically, it can begin at any time of year. If your business operates on a calendar year, your annual bookkeeping begins on

January 1 and ends December 31. If you operate your business on a fiscal year, you begin your 12-month bookkeeping cycle some time after January 1 and end it 12 months after that. The federal government's fiscal year begins October 1. Some business structures, such as sole proprietorships, are required to operate on a calendar year. Whichever way you maintain your books, your business year structure is important for tax issues and to anchor your annual business planning and assessment.

Keeping accurate and detailed books is important. There are many terms and systems, but nothing is as important as committing yourself to fine bookkeeping. You must keep track of all accounts, income, and expenses. This is critical to the health and growth of your company. It is the only way you can know how your business is doing and whether you are meeting projections. It is the method by which you will track the effectiveness of your marketing because your records will tell you where your leads come from, what your closing rate is, how much your average customer spends, which services they need and request, what your materials cost, how much you pay your employees, and all the other small and large details of operating a successful business. Use the best software that offers the most small business support.

12

Advertising the Modern Way

Building a brand around you as the staffing professional or executive recruiter and the specific types of staffing services your business provides involves a myriad of factors, including the spirit, personality, slogan, values, look, feel, and benefits of the company, its representatives, and its services. When building a brand, focus on connecting with the target audience; the brand you build should reflect how you want the target audience to feel when they see your business card, website, or logo. Building a brand is about appealing to all five senses.

To find the essence of your company, the next few sections walk you through the process of uncovering the right look and feel, the right brand, for the staffing service. As you go through the steps, also keep in mind branding flows through to you as the owner and any representatives of your business. The staffing business tends to be based on the experience and skills of the owner or recruiters working the business. In this case, the brand is built around you because, in reality, you are the business.

Character

The first step in the brand process is to determine the character of the company. As a staffing service, how should the business feel and act? What does the business like, and what does it dislike?

A good example of company character is The Walt Disney Co. Disney has created an entire product line and theme parks all based on being the happiest place on earth. Disney's character is fun, whimsical, and magical. This character shines bright in everything Disney does, sells, and supports. From Mickey Mouse to the Cinderella Castle and the giant teacups to spin around in, fun and whimsical are the overriding theme of everything that has anything to do with Disney.

Branding for a staffing service might be more serious than for Disney, but it might not. If a staffing service focuses on the placement of creative professionals, such as writers and graphic designers, it is possible for imagination and fantasy to trickle into the company brand. The character of the staffing service is the foundation for the next step in the brand-building process, which involves the relationship between the business and its customers. This is customer relations. When a customer purchases an alarm system from a security company, he or she feels safe. When someone walks into Disneyland, it makes him or her feel happy, fun, or young again. Which feeling are you trying to conjure up in your clients? Jot down on a piece of paper any adjectives that describe the feelings your business should invoke in your clients.

Aesthetics

When it comes to branding, there is also a visual component; it must be aesthetically pleasing to prospective and current clients. The visual components of branding are the logo, character or mascot, color schemes, and font styles. Visual branding can work one of two ways. First, you might build a relationship with a client, and seeing the visual representations of the company might reinforce the feeling they have about working with your business. Second, a prospective client might see the visual components of the company and either be intrigued enough by what they see to learn more or get turned off by what they see and move on.

In a way, visual branding is similar to meeting someone for the first time. A person might be judged by the way he or she looks, but once you get to know that person, what you see and what you feel might not match. In branding a company, however, it is important that you match the look of the business components with the way you want customers to feel about your company. For example, when you see a big, yellow, bouncing smiley face talking about rolling back prices, visions of Walmart and its low-cost goods probably come to mind.

Think about and write down how your company logo, colors, font styles, and other representations should reflect the values, morals, strengths, and benefits of the staffing service. These representations should trigger instant recognition in prospective and current clients and candidates.

Branding at the level of Walmart, Target, Disney, or Coca-Cola might not be in reach for your staffing business. The key element here is not to create a huge conglomerate in the staffing world but a connection between your staffing service and the people, businesses, or organizations that can benefit from the services it provides.

Now is the time to connect each element of the branding process to create a brand for you as the staffing professional, for the staffing service, and for the services your business provides. The company brand is the bridge between the company and its customers. It is possible to create a bridge that attracts repeat business.

Branding is Perception

Many companies create a brand based on how they want their customers to feel and connect with the company and services. Unfortunately, this is not always the outcome. In reality, a brand is about how current and potential customers perceive it to be. Finding the balance between the way you want your brand to be perceived and the way it is perceived is the key to successful branding.

For example, a nonprofit organization built a brand around helping battered women make it on their own by providing job training, business suits, and interview skills to help them land new jobs and start new lives. Potential donors to the organization, however, thought the organization existed to help an entirely different group of people. Because the perception was different from the reality, the nonprofit continuously struggled with raising enough money to fund its programs and initiatives.

When brand perception is off-balance in a for-profit business situation, it can be even more important because it might mean the difference between running a profitable staffing service and having to close the business forever.

Three Ways to Balance the Brand with Audience Perception

1. Create and write a mission statement for the company people will understand and remember.

2. Survey potential and current clients to see what they think the company does and which services it offers. If this matches the purpose of the company, the brand and brand perception are in balance. If not, adjustments need to be made so the balance is restored.

> **3.** Segment messaging with the audience. No matter which type of staffing service you have, chances are you have several different market segments you cater to. At a minimum, you have clients and candidates. When creating a brand and messaging, make sure it aligns with the audience you are targeting. For example, the messages you send to your potential companies are vastly different than those you would send to candidates.

Customer perception is everything when it comes to branding. You can hire the most expensive branding company in the world to design your logo and create a brand for your business, but if the company brand and customer perception do not match, it is all just a waste of time and money.

Creating a mission statement

One aspect of a company brand is the mission statement. Writing a mission statement mystifies most business owners, but a mission statement is not as baffling as some might think. Understanding the basic purpose of a mission statement makes writing it a simple, fast, and easy process. A mission statement is one or two sentences explaining why the company exists and its purpose and values. If you are drawing a blank when writing a mission statement, these three easy steps will help you break down the writer's block and write a compelling mission statement that does your staffing company justice. *You can see additional information in the discussion of writing a business plan in Chapter 5.*

1. **Focus on purpose:** Many business think the mission of the company has to be long, drawn out, and complicated. This is not true. You can and should be able to describe the reason your company exists and one of the key benefits clients derive from working with the company. Disney is one of the largest companies

in the world, and its mission statement is summed up in four words: "to make people happy."

2. **Focus on fulfillment:** Writing a mission statement and being able to fulfill it are two different things. Writing a mission statement is not about writing it for the sake of writing one. The company also has to have the ability to fulfill the mission statement, so be realistic. For example, an environmental organization might have a mission statement that reads, "to make the world a safer place to live." This statement alone does not have much meaning attached to it because how the company is going about making the world a "safer place to live" is not clear. On the other hand, the Florida organization Save the Manatee Club focuses its international efforts on one area of the world: the water. It chose one animal in the sea world: the manatee. The mission of Save the Manatee: "...to protect endangered manatees and their aquatic habitat for future generations."

3. **Write it down:** The first two steps were thought-provoking processes to encourage you to think about the purpose of your business and how you can go about fulfilling that purpose. Now, put your mission statement into words and down on paper. Keep the mission short, simple, and to the point. Your goal is to be able to hand the mission statement to complete strangers and have all them understand what your company does.

Brand your business for modern times

Before the widespread use of Internet marketing, branding applied to tangible marketing collateral, such as brochures, business cards, and letterheads. Modern times, however, have opened the door to entirely new marketing collateral, such as websites, blogs, and social media networks. Modern times call for modern measures, so here are some branding exercises to walk through when evaluating the company brand online and offline.

Be search engine friendly: Controlling the message current and potential customers see from your business is as important online as it is offline. Who does not sit down at his or her computer and use a search engine to find information out about companies, products, and services? When writing copy for the company website or posting blogs and articles online, make sure to include words in the copy that customers would use to find the staffing services your company provides. You want to control the information someone sees when searching for your business, which is also being in control of the company branding.

Write and post with care: Publishing online is easy to do. In some cases, it is too easy, which can cause a company branding problem. When you write and publish something online, it stays on the Web somewhere forever even if you delete it. Be careful what you say when you post something online. Make sure it reflects what the staffing service stands for and sheds a positive rather than a negative light on your business. Make a good first impression, and avoid racy or potentially problematic photos or statements.

Match tangibles with intangibles: Branding requires consistency. This means the same colors, logo, look, and feel run through all your marketing collateral: website, e-mails, online banner ads, print ads, letterhead, brochures, and business cards.

Personal and company image

In a staffing service, the staffing professional's image and reputation can speak volumes to potential and current clients. If you miss appointments or deliver poor choices for candidates, the client might leave with a bad impression of you and the staffing service. This affects the current client relationship and puts the future relationship in jeopardy. Most individuals and corporate employees refer businesses that have done a good job for them, so make the right impression the first time. It can help you land one client and many more to come.

Image is much more than the way you handle clients. Reputation and professionalism both play an important role in image as well. Ethical behavior and trustworthiness are characteristics clients are willing to pay a higher fee to receive. Creating a good image and reputation is an ongoing process, but there are several things you can do to start off on the right foot.

A Book is Judged by its Cover (and Pages)

Creating a professional image is about what you look like on the outside and the professional way you come across to people when you meet them. Although you might be a genius in your field, if you show up at a client meeting in wrinkled clothing with your hair standing up and coffee on your shirt, your appearance might put clients off. Being a professional starts from the outside and works its way in. Acting in a professional manner also adds to an image. Be aware of using foul language, allowing your bad habits to show, and displaying other rude behaviors you might have. Work on correcting these habits and personality traits even if it means creating a work persona that you put on when you talk to clients on the phone or walk into their office for a meeting.

What to do to Create a Professional Image

- Minimize any negative aspects, such as body language or appearance, that could be misconstrued as unprofessional.

- Be honest with clients. Let them know what you can and cannot do, and be honest about their needs and your ability to fulfill them. This earns the client's respect.

- Dress professionally. Wear what you would expect the client to be wearing or better. If you look sloppy, clients will believe your work is sloppy and might refrain from working with you.

- Under-promise and over-deliver. Do not make promises you cannot keep. Always clearly state what you can and cannot do. It is better to tell a client something cannot be done and then pull it off for them than tell them you can do something you cannot deliver.

- Connect your personal image with the business image using marketing collateral, such as business cards, letterhead, and report covers, that represent you and the company.

Reputation

A reputation is even more important to potential and current clients than image because a bad reputation can damage an image. Several key areas affect the reputation of a staffing professional. The primary element of a reputation is the work quality, which in this case is the quality of the candidates you provide for job positions. Second in importance is the way the staffing professional presents in public. Both of these elements help build a positive, high-quality reputation rather than a negative reputation. It is easier to maintain a good reputation than to have to overcome a bad reputation. Once you do something to hurt your reputation, it takes twice as much work to get back on track, and you might never fully recover. Therefore, taking steps necessary to maintain the best reputation possible is imperative.

One way to build a positive reputation quickly is to always perform your tasks and complete client interactions to the best of your ability. Because the staffing industry or niche you are working in is your passion and area of expertise, this should not be hard to do. Make yourself readily available and easy to talk to, and keep the lines of communication open with your clients. Community involvement can also boost a reputation. Volunteering and working in the community allows you to shape a positive reputation while doing good deeds. If you are starting a staffing service that places tax professionals, offer your services pro bono to nonprofit organizations for a cause you support. Offer a free seminar to teach local tax professionals how to market themselves to potential employers. Write and submit news pieces, editorials, or articles that offer a different and interesting perspective to major newspapers and magazines within your field. Write a book on an aspect of your job and career. Getting your name out to where your customers are is one of the best ways to build a high-quality reputation.

Weaving the Brand Together

Once you determine the look and feel you want to use to represent your personal and company brand, the most important part of branding is weaving it into every aspect of your staffing business. Branding encompasses everything internally and externally. Whether it is a memo that goes around to the employees of the business or an e-mail that you are sending out to the client list, the brand standards apply. Some of the items you need to consider when applying the business brand include:

- Company logo

- Business cards

- E-mail signature

- Letterhead

- Brochures

- Marketing kit

- Website

- Blog

- Mailing envelopes

- Promotional items, such as pens, magnets, notepads, and drink cozies

- Proposals

- Client agreements or contracts

CASE STUDY: NICHE TO BE RICH

Jared Franklin, Owner
Chase Technology Consultants
15 Broad St, First Floor
Boston, MA 02109
(617) 227-5000
www.chasetechconsultants.com

Jared Franklin founded Chase Technology Consultants in April 2007. The firm is a niche technology staffing company that works with clients within Massachusetts, Rhode Island, and New Hampshire. More specifically, Chase Technology Consultants specializes in the permanent, temp-perm, and contract placements of highly skilled technology professionals. Candidates have a salary range between $50,000 and $140,000 with anywhere from one to more than 10 years of professional experience.

The location of Chase Technology Consultants places the firm in the center of two technology markets: MS .NET framework, responsible for the general term web 2.0, and PHP/JAVA, also known as open source technologies. Franklin stresses the importance of staying technically current, relevant, fresh, and on point with the branding of the business to market its staffing services effectively and efficiently. He says dealing with software engineers and developers responsible for many of the most cutting-edge applications has taught him and his employees how to stay on the cutting edge with marketing and branding efforts.

Franklin touts the use of advertisements on various job boards and specialty niche posting sites as one of his most effective forms of advertising. The firm's advertisements on the technology job board, Dice, have been in the top 1 percent for performance, or views to clicks, for two years. Franklin says this is because they spend time writing detailed, specific, clean ads. The firm focuses on marketing the agency as a professional, relevant, committed staffing brand that represents consistency and offers value.

In addition to classified ads on websites and placement boards, Chase Technology Consultants also uses social media platforms. The firm shares relevant and thought-provoking content on its social media platforms to attract new followers and to continuously communicate with existing followers.

Franklin also credits networking, building and maintaining relationships, and communication as part of the company marketing strategy. Although Chase Technology Consultants is a young firm in the market, it embraces this by meeting face to face with its clients and seeing every candidate as a platform for sharing the company's success story. These face to face meetings add a human element to the company by promoting it as a local niche resource committed to being the solution to the hiring pains or needs of its clients.

Franklin points out internal marketing is just as important as external marketing. Chase Technology Consultants invests in its employees and their development. The firm trains all new hires and existing employees through an interactive, hands-on, 45-day training program. This ensures that when employees connect with clients and candidates on the phone or in person, everyone is representing the firm and its brand consistently.

Marketing messaging

To start building a solid marketing foundation, one of the first tasks you will need to tackle is determining your marketing message. A marketing message is the signal you want to send to your current and potential customers about your services. Some marketing professionals refer to this as a **positioning statement** because it is a written statement that positions your company and how you want it to come across to clients.

The efforts discussed throughout the rest of this chapter have two separate components. The first component is how you are going to market or promote your business to client companies. The second component is how you are going to market and promote your business to candidates.

After you get your positioning statement in order, you will want to establish one to three key messages you want to send to current and potential customers through your marketing efforts. These key marketing messages directly promote the services you are touting for your business, but they are not taglines or memorable and catchy phrases. Instead, these are the messages that you want the audience to walk away with after reading your marketing collateral.

To create your own key messages, list the three primary services you plan to offer your clients. Under each service, list out how the service benefits clients. Now form messages with the services and the service benefits that you want clients to walk away with after exposure to your marketing initiatives.

Website

Having a website is an essential component of conducting business these days. Getting your business website up and running boils down to two main options. You can either build and maintain the website yourself or hire a professional to build and maintain it for you.

A myriad of website companies offer templates you can use to customize the look and feel of your business website. Other companies allow you to host your site with them but build it with a desktop publishing or design program, such as Microsoft Publisher or Adobe® Dreamweaver. Taking this route might cost you anywhere from $4.95 per month to about $50 per month depending on the Web host you choose and the service options you choose to use through the host, such as memory storage, e-mail addresses, template options, and domain name.

The other main option is to hire a Web designer to custom design a site for your business. The cost for a custom website design can run you anywhere from $100 for a basic site to thousands of dollars for a complex site. Consider the cost of hiring a designer to create your staffing business site and to make changes to the site after it is up and running.

If it is within your budget, choose a custom site for your initial design. Although this will make any changes and maintenance for the site difficult, you can let the professionals do what they do best: build a well-designed website. After the design of the site is settled, you also have to consider how you are going to obtain the content for the site. You either have to write the content on your own or hire a writer to create the content for you. This can be an added expense of anywhere from $100 to thousands of dollars depending on how many pages of content you need the writer to create for the site.

A basic website for a staffing service has at least four pages. You should have a home page, which provides a brief overview of the type of staffing agency you are and the services you provide. For example, if you are a temp agency, make it clear these are the only types of positions for which you place candidates.

You should also have an About page. This page should discuss the history of the company and the experience of the owner and any staff members who are part of the agency. You should provide a headshot of everyone and information that it illustrates how their expertise benefits both client companies and candidates looking for positions.

The third page is the Services page. This page should list each type of staffing service you provide. A temp service might include information that tells client companies how they act as the human resources and payroll manager for the temp employees so the client company does not have to worry about any of this. If you offer resume services for candidates, list it as part of your offering for candidates.

The final page should be a Contact Us page. This page should include all your contact information, such as phone number, e-mail address, and physical address if you have an office. You might want to have a submission form so visitors can submit their contact information to you and even a way to attach forms, such as resumes or job descriptions.

Brochures

Some staffing professionals — the ones who meet face to face with clients more often or the ones who send physical marketing packages to clients — find it helpful to have a company brochure. Brochures can be used in various marketing initiatives from handing them out at trade shows to including them in marketing kits to media professionals or potential clients. Staffing professionals who focus more on online marketing replace a printed brochure with an electronic option. A third group of staffing professionals uses a combination of an online and printed brochure. You might even have two brochures: one that speaks directly to client companies and a completely separate brochure that speaks to potential candidates.

As is the case with creating a logo, you can design and print brochures for your staffing business in a variety of ways. The most expensive way to obtain brochures is to hire a graphic designer to make it and then send the file off to a printer to have the brochures printed.

Vistaprint and 48hourprint.com also provide customizable brochure templates and printing options. These sites allow you to design your own brochure, add the content, and print the quantity you need at a reduced rate compared to most local printers. You can also opt to have the brochure designed by a professional or use desktop publishing software to create your own brochure layout and then upload the design to one of these websites to print the brochures.

Finally, you can buy brochure card stock that is scored for folding at your local office supply or stationery store. Use a desktop publishing program or templates to customize your brochures, and print them using your home computer and printer. Although this method can be highly cost-effective and you can print brochures as you need them rather than ordering hundreds or thousands at a time, make sure the brochures do not lose their professional appearance. If your brochure looks anything less than professional, it might turn clients away from working with you.

Marketing kits

To get potential clients to buy service-based and high-ticket items such as staffing, you have to impress them more than a product-based business. Putting together a marketing kit provides your staffing business with the opportunity to impress, motivate, and sell by giving your audience more information than is possible to fit on a business card or in a brochure or to say in an elevator pitch.

Marketing kits can be a powerful tool to convert sales; leave the kit after a client meeting, or drop it in the mail as a follow-up to a phone conversation or in response to a prospect's e-mail request for more information. Always include two business cards and a company brochure if you have one. There are a few key essentials needed for your marketing kit:

Folder: To build a marketing kit, you need a folder or some sort of holder for the marketing information. The container the marketing kit comes in is the first impression your prospects receives, so you want it to look professional. You can accomplish this in one of two ways. First, you have the option of having folders professionally printed for less with online printers. A less expensive option is to have a professionally printed label that you can affix to a linen pocket folder you purchase at any major office supply store.

Marketing template: To weave the staffing company brand through all the marketing pieces, you will next want to create a marketing template. A marketing template is the layout each piece is printed on.

USP: Earlier in this book, you learned about creating a unique selling proposition to make your staffing business stand out from competitors. Make sure your USP is included as part of the marketing kit information. Word it so it shows how your company can benefit customers from the customer's point of view.

Sell the benefits: Most businesses provide a list of features rather than the benefits a client enjoys by working with their company. When you list a staffing service in your marketing kit, make sure you are listing out how this service benefits the client by revealing how it resolves an issue.

Service offering: Include a bulleted list that allows the client to see your service offering at a quick glance. Follow the bulleted list with a more descriptive list of the staffing services your company offers.

Testimonials: Client testimonials can sell your services better than anything you can say to prospects. Include a full page of client testimonials, or have your clients record testimonials that you then include on a DVD or CD as part of the marketing kit.

Articles or media coverage: Third-party endorsements from the media can also pack a powerful sales punch and should be included in the marketing kit. Include reprints of articles published about your company; DVDs of media interviews; or newspaper, magazine, and online article clips in which you have been quoted as an expert source or your staffing business mentioned.

Now that you have the foundational tools ready for marketing the staffing business, the next chapter covers how to attract clients to the staffing business.

Writing the Marketing Plan

The marketing plan is the action part of your business; these are steps you can proactively take to promote the business, make people aware the business exists, and find new clients. *Your marketing plan is what you wrote in the Marketing Strategies section of the Business Plan in Chapter 5.* There are two sides to every marketing plan, which covers online and offline tactics you can use as a staffing professional to attract the clients that fall into your target market and be hired by those clients. You can use the marketing plan as-is to get started. Marketing plans are dynamic documents because after you implement the plan, you have to go back and evaluate the success or failure of your marketing tactics. Once you analyze the results, you tweak and adjust the marketing plan for implementation during the next six months or year.

Marketing a staffing business is a process. You cannot conduct a marketing activity one time but decide that it is a complete failure because you do not see immediate results. You must take consistent action in implementing your marketing strategies for at least six months to a year.

The first part of the marketing plan is the marketing strategy. For a staffing business, three marketing strategies exist. Commit these three strategies to memory because every marketing activity covered in the remainder of the plan hinges on these three strategies.

1. Gather qualified leads and followers to grow your subscriber list and database.

2. Nurture the qualified leads and followers in your database by consistently getting in front of them, in various ways, with information about your staffing services.

3. Convert the leads into clients and generate revenue by introducing them to your staffing services.

Marketing foundation

Before you can start to implement and integrate the various marketing activities set forth in the marketing plan, you first have to build your marketing foundation. Because the first half of the marketing plan covers the online activities you can use to attract clients, the staffing business website needs to be up and fully functioning so you have a venue to drive traffic to when marketing your staffing services online.

To build the brand of the staffing business, include a few implementation strategies as part of the website to grab the attention of your ideal client. Traffic should be driven to the website from a variety of venues, which will be discussed later in the plan. Driving traffic to the home page of the website will be an important first step to gathering leads and converting them into clients. It will set the stage for learning more about these prospects and then up-selling them into the next logical service level you offer that fits their needs.

By incorporating certain elements into your Web design, you can increase the credibility of your staffing site, which allows you to gather highly targeted leads that can be further qualified and turned into more revenue for the business. The following are elements your website should include:

Entice with an irresistible free offer: Offer an incentive to help capture information on the visitors to your website. An irresistible free offer might be a free downloadable report on a topic of interest to them. In exchange for the visitors to your site providing their name and e-mail address to you, provide something to them for free. Capturing these leads is the key to building your database of prospective clients. If visitors to your site are interested in accepting your free gift in exchange for providing you with their information, they are potential clients for your business at least initially. The rest of your marketing activities help you to further qualify these leads and eventually move them into client status.

Another free offer could be a CD or DVD for candidates on how to ace the job interview. If you are trying to attract client companies, you could offer a free report, webinar, or CD that provides the top characteristics to look for in the best candidates.

The point of the free offer is to position yourself as an expert in the staffing industry. You want to provide them with enough information to reveal your expertise, but at the end of reading the report, listening to the CD, or watching the DVD, they should see or hear an offer or incentive that makes them want to hire you to handle their staffing services for them.

Further qualify subscribers: As part of the subscription process, add a one-question survey to the free offer subscription. Use a question that directly relates to the challenges your clients might face. For example, a staffing service might ask, "What is your biggest challenge or obstacle in landing the perfect employees?" The point of the question is to find out what your prospects are thinking, feeling, or seeking information about. You can then use the information you gather to create solutions that cater directly to what clients and prospects are looking for.

Ensure comprehensive branding: Make sure your branding is carried throughout all your Web pages, auto-responders, and other marketing collateral for the sake of consistency. Use the same color schemes, font styles, layouts, and templates throughout all your materials.

Optimize your pages: Use keywords in the copy of your website that prospective clients would use to search for the products or services your staffing business offers; this is the basis of search engine optimization (SEO). Choose one or two keywords to focus on for each page of your site, and then scatter the keywords, phrase, and combinations of the phrase in the beginning, in the middle, and toward the end of your copy. Make sure the copy is written to include the keywords so text flows and sounds natural. You can use free keyword tools, such as the Google AdWords Keyword Tool, or you can hire a professional keyword or SEO professional to help you come up with a list of keywords to include on the site.

If you provide services to a confined geographic area, be sure to include keywords that speak about the area you cover. You should also use the keywords in the page titles, headlines, and subheads in the copy on each page.

Internet Marketing and List-building

A growing business requires you to steadily grow your existing database by gathering highly targeted new leads. This creates the foundation for significant business growth and increased revenue for your staffing business. Once you fill your database with the ideal prospects you seek, you can then work on selling them your fee-based products and services by communicating with them on a regular basis. Here are some ways to keep your clients up to date:

E-newsletter: Regularly publish an e-mail newsletter to create an automatic lead-capturing system online and as a communication tool for your existing database. You can provide how-to articles, tips, and advice for candidates on landing the career of their dreams. You can also include news on the employment rate or industry news if you specialize in a specific industry or niche. You might even list open positions you are trying to fill, workshops you are offering, or other information that pertains to candidates looking for employment.

You can provide similar information to your client employees. You can provide how-to articles, tips, and advice on how to interview and hire the right employees. You can keep them up-to-date on changes in employment laws or industry news on employment rates or regulations for the industry in which the business operates.

Both newsletters might even include case studies on candidates or clients you have been able to help. Of course, you will need to keep your client and candidate mailing lists separate.

Editorial calendar: Create an editorial calendar to map out discussion topics for the next six weeks or so. Block out time on your calendar each week to create this content for your newsletters. You can also use existing content, such as products, presentations, and reports, to break down and turn into articles and sections of the newsletter. Each article or tip you include in the newsletter should be about 200 to 400 words. The editorial calendar can also be used for creating blog posts if you decide to start and run a blog and social media updates.

Social media

Harnessing the power of social media outlets drives more targeted traffic to your website, which in turn will drive more clients to your staffing business. This provides you with the opportunity to communicate with your target market on a more regular basis and in different ways, and it can have a powerful and positive effect on growing your list and your staffing business. Social media networks include Facebook, Twitter, LinkedIn, and YouTube. Each social media network works slightly differently, so you will need to familiarize yourself with each one. The following sections, however, go into detail on how you can use each network as part of your social media marketing efforts. You can implement the following social media strategies:

Facebook Fan Page

Create a Facebook fan page that speaks directly to your target markets and focuses on the geographic area of your business if applicable. On the fan page for your business, you can also include an opt-in box for your free offer so visitors can immediately subscribe to your list and be taken to your website. To build your fan base, include a special announcement in your e-newsletter to drive traffic to the fan page. Be sure to include a link to your fan page in every piece of correspondence you have with your prospects and client. This way, you are creating a two-way street to drive traffic between social media and your website. If you can gather video or audio testimonials from clients, these are also ways to let your services speak for themselves. If not, record case studies or scenarios in which you can illustrate how your service helped a client gain success.

You can use the Facebook fan page in various ways, including sharing your blog posts with links to drive prospective and current clients directly to where the post sits on your site and posing questions to your audience in an effort to engage them and make it more of an interactive experience. This also allows you to evaluate who your audience is on your fan page so you can then work on funneling them into the appropriate service level of your business.

If you find the majority of your fan base is from financial service companies, this might be an indication this industry is having a hard time finding candidates because they are the ones most interested in your services. It might also show you already specialize in this industry. If not, it might be a niche you should consider. You can also integrate your Twitter™ account with your fan page so your updates get more exposure. Use a custom background that matches your brand in addition to the sidebar information about your business. A dramatic or attractive background can boost interest for followers.

Because Facebook limits actual profiles to individuals, it is better practice to create a Facebook fan page or group for your staffing business and integrate your personal Facebook profile with your business's page. Use your personal profile page to talk about your professional relation to the business, join relevant groups, and RSVP to events that connect to your target market. Join groups or become a fan of any professional organizations you belong to and any of your competitors. Also, integrate your Twitter account with your profile so your updates get more exposure.

Twitter

Twitter is another social media marketing tool you can use to promote your staffing business online. Use Twitter to share information and services related to your business. This helps position you as an expert resource for information without always trying to sell them on your products and services. Aim for 80 percent information sharing and 20 percent promotion.

An example tweet might say, "Ad agency seeks witty writing pro in financial service industry www.xyz.com." Another example might be, "Looking for marketing pro that can boost your website visitors through the roof? www.xyz.com"

You can integrate your tweets with your blog posts and articles, which is a highly effective way to attract followers and permits you to communicate with your followers and drive them to your website or blog. Almost all tweets should include a link to a specific blog article, product, or service on your website. Sharing helpful tips on how to hire successful employees or how a candidate can land the job of his or her dreams on Twitter has to be done within the 140 characters that Twitter allows for tweets. Make your tweets intriguing, and then send your followers somewhere they can get more information by including a link. Twitter allows you to share information, but your goal is to use it as a tool to drive traffic to your staffing website, which is also the goal with all your social media marketing. Be sure to use short URLs on Twitter to keep the length of your tweet short. Bitly (**http://bitly.com**) is a URL shortener that also tracks your links and gives you information on how active a certain post is.

Follow people you admire, such as authors, bloggers, e-zines you read, seminars you attend, or leaders in your field, and your competitors. Visit these profiles and their lists of followers to find people to follow who fit your target market. Consider having a custom background created that matches your brand in addition to the sidebar information about your business. A dramatic or attractive background can boost interest for followers.

LinkedIn®

LinkedIn is another online source for professionals, business owners, and entrepreneurs that can develop your staffing services. Add a direct link to your website's home page in your profile so people can take advantage of your free offer right away. Your LinkedIn profile should connect to your blog for further exposure of your content. You can start connecting with individuals in related businesses. This is a way to connect with possible joint venture partners, potential clients, and other referral sources. Also look for people located in the geographic area your business covers if applicable.

LinkedIn provides a built-in application for gathering recommendations from clients you have worked with or other professionals on LinkedIn you have done business with. Spend some time once per quarter gathering recommendations from your contacts. LinkedIn can be a powerful tool, especially after you have connected with at least 500 other professionals. Even if you cannot get recommendations, you need to use LinkedIn as a tool to connect with your target audiences.

YouTube®

Create and use a free YouTube account to upload instructional videos that speak on your target audience's interests, such as how to ace an interview. You can also turn each of your written blog posts and e-newsletter articles into a video. You are providing just enough information to encourage your audience to gain more information by going to your website. These videos can also be added to your Facebook profile and fan page for additional exposure.

You want to be everywhere your target audience is, and these are the social media websites your target market is using.

CASE STUDY: MARKET
TO YOUR TARGET

Annie Davis, Owner
Annie's Nannies Household Staffing
2236 58th St., Suite 101
Seattle, WA 98107
(206) 784-8462
www.anihouseholdstaffing.com

Annie's Nannies Household Staffing finds all household staff for families, which includes full-time, part-time, ongoing, long-term, short-term, and temporary positions. The firm also works on staffing special events. Annie Davis began the agency when she saw a need for childcare service providers, such as nannies. As the needs of her clients changed and expanded, Davis expanded the staffing services to provide other household positions.

Annie's Nannies Household Staffing started in a home office in 1984. As the firm grew and expanded, Davis obtained office space. She now owns the building in which the firm runs, so employees have a space to work in and meet in every day. Since the firm first began, the need for office space is not the only change that Davis has experienced. She also says advertising to reach both clients and candidates is a whole new realm.

The advertising efforts for Annie's Nannies Household Staffing relies primarily on the Internet. The firm often posts ads to attract potential clients and candidates on Craigslist, Facebook, and other social networking sites. All these advertising methods also allow the agency to rely on the most reliable form of marketing of all times: word of mouth. Word-of-mouth advertising can easily spread in the online environments the agency has established but is also a viable option offline.

The agency does run some print ads. These ads are primarily targeted at clients, or the households that would have an interest in hiring staff. In addition to this, Davis sends out a quarterly newsletter. She and her staff maintain a list of previous clients, prospects who have inquired about their services, and even clients who are currently using the firm for placement. The newsletter shares information about the company and the staffing industry, and it also lists any special promotions the firm is running at the time.

Blog

Having an up-to-date blog is one of the primary ways people are going to find your staffing business online because search engines look for updated content when determining page rank. Share your expertise about your business, industry, or niche in your blog posts. Then, integrate your blog with the social media sites, including Facebook, LinkedIn, and Twitter, to help drive traffic to your site. Mix it up between longer, more wordy posts talking about industry specific news and shorter posts about a new product or service. Any videos or images you can add will also help make your blog more three-dimensional. Your blog should not be just about your business. You want to connect with your clients, not hard sell them your services. You can use complimentary blogging platforms, such as Wordpress (**www.wordpress.com**) or Blogger (**www.blogger.com**) to create and maintain a blog.

For a blog to be an effective marketing tool, post on your blog at least two to three times a week. Blog posts should include keywords your potential clients and target markets use to find information on the services you provide. You can also map out a year's worth of e-newsletter content, tweets, and public relations campaigns that are all built around the same editorial content topics to keep everything aligned.

Article marketing

Use content you have created and develop it into new articles. Aim for at least one article per week. Popular topics for staffing professionals include how-to articles and articles that cover specific steps or detailed information on topics relevant to your audience. A staffing professional might write an article on the top five ways to customize a résumé to fit the job in which the applicant is interested.

You can use these articles to disseminate information on your e-newsletter. Upload them to article directories, such as EzineArticles (**www.ezinearticles.com**) and Amazines (**www.amazines.com**). Use them on your blog, and post them on your social media networks. Make sure your articles are also rich with keywords. Article marketing is one of the most effective and least expensive ways to drive targeted traffic to your staffing website. Your goal in using article marketing is to drive visitors to the appropriate page of your site where your free offer sits. Your goal is to get them to request the free offer in exchange for gathering their information. You do this by including a strong call to action in the resource box of each article you submit online. This also leads to other marketing communication efforts and up-selling to your paid services.

You can record the articles you write and repurpose them into videos and podcasts. Upload the podcasts to your blog and create an audio or video series that you can include on your blog, distribute in your e-newsletter, upload to YouTube, or send out as a special series of e-mail blasts to your subscriber list. Podcasts can also be uploaded and distributed on iTunes.

Link building

On a weekly basis, visit the websites, blogs, and forums related to your business, niche, or industry. These are additional places where your audience is looking for information, and they are another place where you can find information and build relationships with other staffing companies. Post a relevant, valuable comment on at least five sites per week. Forums and blog posts allow you to post your name, business name, and a link back to your site, which drives traffic back to your website. This is an indirect way of promoting your business by positioning yourself as an expert and a resource while creating additional exposure for your business. You want your name, company name, and Web address all over the sites that have anything to do with your business. If your potential clients are visiting these sites, you want them to see you there, too.

Sites of this nature might also offer an opportunity for you to become a guest author or article contributor, which allows you to use content you have to share your expertise with a new audience, gain the attention of your target market by positioning yourself as the expert you are, and broaden your reach.

Direct response

You also need to focus on nurturing the existing leads you have and the new ones you are gathering by consistently communicating with your database. You can communicate with your database by sending out auto-responders and promotional e-mails at least once or twice a month. Promotional e-mails might include a special offer on one of your staffing services, announce the dates of an upcoming webinar, or incorporate a case study that illustrates a problem one of your clients faced and how your services resolved the problem. Promotions and case studies can also be included in the e-newsletter.

Traditional Marketing is Not Dead

Now that you have a variety of ways you can market your staffing business online, take a look at the avenues available for marketing your business offline.

List building

Although there are numerous ways you can build your list using online marketing tactics, there are just as many ways you can build your list with offline marketing tactics. The best way to build your list is to combine your online and offline efforts. Some of the ways you can build your list offline include:

- Be a guest or participate in as many webinars as possible.
- Be a regular guest on various Internet radio shows.
- Advertise with organizations and associations targeting your ideal clients.
- Interview well-known people in your niche and post these interviews online and in print publications.
- Submit articles to print publications your target market reads.

- Advertise in print publications your target market reads.

- Add your free irresistible offer to the back of your business card.

- Do a postcard mailing to a high-quality mailing list.

- Attend live networking events and seminars that cater to your target market.

- Periodically ask past and current clients for referrals.

Public relations program

One of the key programs that will help boost your business and subscriber list while increasing credibility is publicity. Publicity is a low-cost, effective way to reach your target audience. The purpose of publicity for a staffing business is:

- To inform potential clients and referral sources about you, your company, your services, and the ways you can help them.

- To educate the media and potential clients to shape attitudes and behaviors and change perceptions about the staffing industry.

- To effectively communicate your marketing messages.

Public relations (PR) is one of the easiest, most cost-effective ways to promote who you are and what you do so you can get more clients and more sales for your business. It is a marketing effort that builds credibility and visibility to help you gain new clients and increase your income. The art of building favorable and profitable interest in you, your business, or your services by creating a buzz in the marketplace is what public relations is all about. It is a way of getting your message across to tell others about you, what you do, and why it is important to them. Public relations lends credibility to you and builds your reputation from a third-party point of view. It is often more valuable than advertising alone. It is an effective form of marketing because it:

- Creates awareness of your brand.
- Communicates the benefits of your products and services.
- Positions you as an expert.
- Generates sales and leads.

PR is free and lends more credibility to your claims than paid advertisements. It is the most cost-effective way to generate interest about your staffing business and reach existing and potential clients. When people read about you in the media from a journalist or hear about you on the radio, you get instant third-party validation and receive positioning as an expert in your field. Although a paid advertisement placed in a publication can cost you tens of thousands of dollars each time it runs, a well-placed article is much more cost-effective and adds value to your business.

Trade publications have a number of subscribers, and most have thousands of readers. Each is a prospect who might need the services your staffing business offers. The readers at least are likely know someone who needs the services you provide. In addition, this positions you as an expert, which produces a premium price for your services because people are willing to pay more for your expertise. This often removes price as an obstacle to overcome in the process of attracting new clients. PR also levels the playing field and allows small businesses to appear larger than they are and compete at the same level as larger businesses.

PR helps you attract qualified prospects and leads. The more people know about you, the higher the level of trust is built, which makes it more likely they will contact you and refer others to you. As an added bonus, current clients get the confirmation they need that your business is the best one to do business with. Here is how to get started:

Develop a media list: A media list should include local and national outlets that will have an interest in covering your story. Find individual reporters, journalists, and writers for the publication that would have an interest in covering your story. You will need to gather and maintain a PR contact list for these local journalists and publications either by paying for these subscriptions or doing independent research online.

Implement editorial calendars: Most print publications publish a calendar, called an editorial calendar, outlining topics they will be covering throughout the year. Use the editorial calendars of your top media outlets to help you develop story ideas for promoting your business. These lists are useful when pitching story ideas because you can tie your story into these topics. Also monitor and identify publicity opportunities from journalists. Check Help a Reporter Out (**http://helpareporter.com**), PitchRate (**http://pitchrate.com**), and Reporter's Source (**www.reporterssource.com**). By responding to a reporter's source query, you are establishing yourself as an expert in your staffing niche. Your credibility and reputation can only build if you are positively quoted in a news article.

Write a pitch: Your pitch should be personalized to the writer you are pitching the story to. Mention similar stories he or she has covered, or point out why his or her readers would be interested in the story you have to tell. The pitch should also include an overview of the story and an attached press release for more details.

To start, determine the top three local media outlets for newspaper, TV, and radio in the area in which you run your staffing business. Send press releases to specific journalists or editors, and follow up accordingly.

Write a monthly press release. You should send out one press release per month for special events, workshops, or webinars you are promoting. An easy strategy if you do not have something specific to promote for the month is to use your blog or monthly e-newsletter articles as a press release. This way, you leverage your writing and are able to use your content in multiple places and for multiple purposes.

When writing a press release for online media, the main goal is to have search engines pick up your keywords. An SEO press release is geared toward specific keywords rather than a specific story idea. SEO press releases are written and used online to increase the amount of traffic you drive to your website. Keyword-focused press releases are generally distributed through wire services. Many companies, especially larger ones, are sending press releases through these online services for the primary purpose of driving traffic to their websites. Submit your monthly press releases to the top five online press release distribution sites, which include one paid service and four free services.

ONLINE PRESS RELEASE DISTRIBUTION CHANNELS	
PRWeb.com	$80/release
I-newswire.com	Free
IdeaMarketers.com	Free
Free-press-release.com	Free
24-7pressrelease.com	Free

Pitch to the media and follow up frequently: Once a month when you write the press release, pitch the story to the appropriate media outlets. Follow up with each media contact you have pitched the story to, and make sure they received the information. Use the follow-up as an opportunity to see whether they are interested in covering the story.

Speaking opportunities

Speaking opportunities can be an excellent source for new prospects and sale conversions for a staffing professional. You can use speaking opportunities to expand your reach and position yourself as an expert in your field. Off-site speaking engagements help you reach potential clients while enforcing the establishment of your expertise. Some options include being a guest speaker for radio shows, webinars, and workshops online or live.

Speaking engagements allow staffing professionals to connect face to face with current and potential clients and referral sources. It provides the opportunity to showcase areas of expertise, schedule appointments with potential clients and candidates, and even close sales.

Have a system in place to gather the names and contact information of the attendees of the show or event at which you are speaking. Run a contest to gather names, e-mail addresses, and telephone numbers. This allows you to build your list of leads and provides you with the opportunity to follow up with those leads to try to convert them into clients. Speaking engagements are also prime locations for selling services on the spot. Run a show or speaking engagement special so if a prospect becomes a client at the show, he or she receives a special discount or bonus offer.

13

When You Want to Exit the Business — or Retire

At some point in the future, you will want to leave your business. You will either be ready to retire or will want to sell the business and move on. When you are ready to sell, it is important to have a profitable, salable business. Even when you start your business, you should be thinking about your exit.

You can build a profitable staffing business with a loyal customer base and an efficient business structure that earns top dollar when you sell. You should consider the fact that with a staffing business, if you remain the only staffing professional, you are the most prized asset. You will not have inventory and equipment as assets, but you will have the loyal customer base and the solid business reputation you built for your staffing agency.

Exit Plan

Now is the time to develop an exit plan. You will not need as much detail for the exit plan as you needed for your business plan, but you want to develop it now and review it each year so you can make any changes necessary. Your business situation will inevitably change from year to year, and you will want to revise. Here are some of the basic items your plan should cover:

- **Your best-case scenario**: Do you know when you want to retire? Decide whether you want to sell the business or leave it for your family to manage.

- **Current value**: If you were to sell your business today, what would it be worth?

- **Enhancing business value**: Which changes would make your business more appealing for a buyer? Consider these carefully, and realize there might be some changes you do not want to make but that will enhance the value of the business when it is time to sell.

- **Worst-case scenario**: If you had to get out of the business today, what could be done?

- **Preparing for the sale**: You will want to be aware of the tax implications of the sale.

- **Leaving**: Are you in a partnership or corporation with others, and if so, how does this affect leaving your business?

- **Financial health for your family**: Prepare a will. Is your family trained and prepared to run the business without you?

Meet with your attorney and your CPA for advice about how to create a realistic exit plan. To see some examples of exit plans, go to:

- American Express® Small Business: **www.openforum.com/ idea-hub/topics/money/article/selling-your-business-consider- these-alternative-exit-strategies-shira-levine**

- Principal Financial Group®: **www.principal.com/businessowner/ bus_exit.htm**

- Family Business Experts: **www.family-business-experts.com/ exit-planning.html**

CASE STUDY: PLAN YOUR ROAD TO SUCCESS

Patty DeDominic, Owner
DeDominic & Associates
2353 East Valley Road
Santa Barbara, CA 93108
(805) 565-9967
www.dedominic.com

Before opening her consulting business, Patty DeDominic was the former owner and CEO of two staffing firms. The first staffing firm was PDQCAREERS, which DeDominic founded. The second staffing form was one she purchased just one month before Sept. 11.

Back in 1979 when she started PDQ, there were few business plans available to new business owners, so DeDominic sketched out some sales forecasts and began working the leads pile the company had. The firm eventually grew. The company even placed some employees and staff with some of the top employers in the country.

DeDominic says nothing is wrong with working without a business plan; Thinking past the day-to-day operations so business owners can focus on the big picture is simply more professional.

Eventually, PDQCAREERS grew to more than 600 employees. Through the years, the original sales forecasts turned into a written and formal business plan. Growth came once the firm wrote a more sophisticated business plan. For example, without a business plan, sales for the company went from $136,000 to $300,000. From the $300,000 mark, the company went on to make $500,000 and then $1 million. At this point, DeDominic and her team could see stepping back and taking time to plan with the company managers and outside advisors was a useful investment. When systems planning and a needs assessment into the business were made, formally recording the plans permitted the company to grow in sales by more than 30 percent.

Part of the formal plan also included an exit strategy and a book put together by the company's investment banker. The planning and using the plan as a guide paid off because PDQCAREERS was sold in 2006 to SELECT Staffing. SELECT Staffing went on to make additional staffing firm acquisitions and become a $1-billion firm. PDQCAREERS sold to SELECT Staffing at just under $30 million in sales.

According to DeDominic, amateurs work hard, but pros plan well and then execute the plan.

Leaving Your Business to a Family Member

Families operate millions of large and small businesses. Some owners pass their business down to family members or heirs. Another option is to pass or sell the business to your business partners or employees.

Leaving the business to a family member has tax implications. These issues include inheritance tax, trusts, and tax-free gifts. Each of these issues has its own set of complications, and you should consult with your attorney, banker, estate planner, and CPA to make sure they are handled well. More resources include:

- The U.S. Chamber of Commerce offers advice at **www.uschamber.com**.
- CCH® Business Owner's Toolkit has articles to help you at **www.toolkit.com**.

Selling to Your Employees

You might not have family members interested in carrying on the business without you, so you might consider selling the business to your employees. They would need to have adequate financing, and you would want to make it a professional transaction and include your attorney or accountant. Be aware this can be highly emotional because the employees buying your business might have different plans and ideas for how to change your business. The other issue is it might feel uncomfortable to negotiate money issues with friends or co-workers.

Your employees might want to talk with a professional so they clearly understand the transaction. For advice see:

- The National Center for Employee Ownership at **www.nceo.org**.
- The Beyster Institute for Entrepreneurial Ownership at **http://rady.ucsd.edu/beyster**.

There are many ways to handle this transaction, including transferring your business to a worker co-op or transferring directly to employees. This is similar to transferring it to family members, so getting advice and understanding the process is good for everyone's sake.

Conclusion

Starting and operating a staffing service can without a doubt be a gratifying and lucrative career move on your part. You have the ability to work with people by helping them find jobs and careers and making a financial impact on their lives and you will also be a business owner. Millions of small business owners branch out on their own each year, and when you decide to take the leap, it can also be a personally and professionally satisfying move.

Running your staffing service the right way also creates a highly profitable situation. You now have all the information you need to get a piece of the $61.8-billion staffing industry. Staffing services are no longer seen as employment agencies for temporary employees and administrative staff seeking positions. They now extend to placing various types of employees with different types of companies. They offer variety and sophistication in addition to providing employers with employees and staff. Whether a company is hesitant to hire employees in a recession or desperate to fill openings in an expansion, the staffing industry provides professional help fulfilling these needs. This book encompasses everything you need to open and operate a staffing service business.

Now that you have read through the book once, go back through and implement each of the steps. Start back at the beginning of the book, complete each step, fill out each of the worksheets, and complete the tasks to start and run your own staffing service business. You have everything you need at your fingertips. It is now up to you to put all this information to good use.

A

What is Included on the CD-ROM

Sample business plan for a staffing/recruiting firm

Essential elements:

1. Executive summary
2. Market analysis
3. Company description
4. Organization and management
5. Marketing and sales management
6. Services and products to be offered
7. Financials
8. Funding requests if asking for loan

This example plan will make some assumptions, such as your structure, financials, and equipment needs. Your specific plan must reflect your needs, marketing conditions, funding, and the advice you receive from your attorney and accountant.

Executive summary

Financial Professionals for You Inc. is an executive recruiting agency serving the tri-county area of South Florida (Miami-Dade, Broward, Palm Beach counties). The focus of the executive recruiting efforts is in the financial services industry. The company works with various types of financial companies, including investment firms, insurance agencies, banks, and other financial institutions, to match specifically skilled financial workers with clients. Financial Professionals for You Inc. will target mid- to large-sized companies with operations in the South Florida area. Even with the recent economic downturn, financial company operations in South Florida remain strong, and the demand for employees with financial experience at various levels of the organization are in high demand, which offers growth opportunities.

Financial Professionals for You Inc. will begin as a corporation owned 100 percent by Jane B. Professional. Jane has worked as an in-house executive recruiter for the past eight years for Miami Investment Pros and more recently as an executive recruiter for KPM Staffing Consultants.

Financial Professionals for You will open for business at the beginning of the year, which is a high-volume time for employees to make career moves. During the first few months in business, Jane will start and operate the business on her own. Jane estimates her own workweek at 60 to 80 hours. If business warrants, Jane will hire a part-time worker for administrative assistance.

Jane forecasts initial business at five to ten medium- to large-sized company clients that have an immediate need for filling open job positions. An additional five to ten other clients will have ongoing hiring needs throughout the year *and on a long-term basis. The average placement fee will be 20 percent of the annual salary of the financial professional plus benefits. Salaries for these professionals range from $35,000 to $250,000 per year. Anticipated monthly revenues during the first year in business are expected to be $12,500. Based on established relationships Jane has, significant placement opportunities are expected during the first year of business; however, we will also continue to market aggressively for additional clients. Our revenues for the first year are forecast at $150,000.*

The summary explains the thinking that justifies the company and its future.

Market analysis

The financial services industry is currently operating in a market for which the need for experienced professionals is growing. First, many of the tenured professionals are retiring, which is opening up higher-level positions within these companies. Second, most of the financial services companies do not have someone in the company who is dedicated to the staffing and hiring needs of the organization. Without someone experienced in identifying and recruiting qualified professionals and someone who is dedicated to the company needs on a full-time and ongoing basis, it is difficult for the companies to find the qualified individuals they seek. These companies have the financial resources to pay for recruiting services and have little desire and lack the resources to do this type of work themselves. The counties expect more than 300 positions at financial companies and at various levels to open up during the next 12 months. Jane will target all these companies, so our estimate of five to ten customers is modest. We expect to exceed that number quickly.

Explain the market you intend to pursue.

Company description

Here, you will formally explain the business structure you have selected. You are, for the purpose of this example, a corporation. In your specific case, you might choose something else. In this portion of your business plan, you would explain it and state your officers and managers.

Organization and management

This is where you will be specific about how your company will be operated. Jane will be owner and executive recruiter. If she plans to hire someone to handle the bookkeeping, she would mention it here. If Jane's office will be at home, she would state that here. Be specific. Personnel and sales goals can also be mentioned and will be expanded on later in this plan.

Marketing and sales management

Financial Professionals for You Inc. will rely primarily on warm and cold call marketing during its first quarter. Jane will contact her existing contacts to let them know she has opened her own agency. She will also distribute fliers and brochures to the office managers and human resources departments of the 300 financial firms operating in the tri-county area. Each office will receive the flier and brochure at least twice. Jane will hire someone to deliver the fliers the first time but will deliver the fliers herself the second time so she can try to start conversations with the individuals responsible for hiring for various positions in the office. She will also ask whether the fliers can be placed into individual financial advisers' mailboxes because these individuals are often responsible for hiring their own support staff.

This is where the plan meets the real world. Think this through, and understand that this is the key part of your plan to make your business successful. All your research and planning will focus on sales and marketing. Explain an entire year's worth of market planning: canvassing, networking, yellow page ads, professional organizations, and any other advertising you plan to use.

Do not expect miracles from your marketing. Fliers generate 1 to 2 percent responses. Out of every 100 fliers you put out, you will get one or two calls. You should close more than half of these responses. The response rate goes up with frequency. Each time a potential customer sees your flier, he or she is more likely to respond. Everything you do will add up to a total marketing strategy that will bring customers to your business.

Services and products

Here, you expand on what you will do for your customers. You need to determine how much income you can project for your services given the number of customers you can realistically expect during your first six months or year.

All your services must be researched. You need to be aware of your competition, their prices, and the market.

Financials

Here is where you make your financial projections for your first three years. These are estimates based on solid information and market conditions, but as with all business activities, nothing is guaranteed. This is still a financial blueprint.

First, make a column of all the services you plan to offer. Forecast sales for them.

Service	2011	2012	2013
Service ex. 1	$7,500	$10,000	$12,500
Service ex. 2	$42,000	$50,000	$55,000

List all your services and what you reasonably expect them to bill.

Next, list your costs. These would include cost of goods but not capital expenses, such as equipment; rent; phone; marketing; insurance; fuel; and other costs of doing business.

Costs

Phone	$600	$625	$700
Insurance	$2,000	$2,100	$2,200
Ads and marketing	$5,000	$6,000	$8,000
Fuel	$1,800	$2,000	$2,000

Make a good faith effort at predicting your costs. Your actual expenses might be higher or lower than your initial projections, so track your expenses monthly to allow for adjustments. You might increase or decrease your marketing expenses according to projected costs versus actual expenses.

Labor

Here is where you list your labor expenses. How much are you going to pay yourself and your part-time employee(s)? If you have employees, you must pay unemployment insurance, workers' compensation insurance, and possibly other fees depending on your state's laws. If a client company hires employees from the candidates you send to the company, the company is responsible for paying for unemployment insurance, workers' compensation insurance, and possibly other fees depending on your state's laws.

Startup costs

List here what you expect the cost of opening your business will be.

Funding requests

If you are going to borrow the money needed to start the business, you must provide a detailed financial statement in addition to the information you already have in your business plan. This is the same information you would provide for any substantial loan from a bank or other financial institution. You must provide assurance you can and will pay back the loan and offer a form of security. This might be your home or other assets, such as savings, stocks, or real estate. Your business and its assets will be part of the security package.

If you are purchasing a franchise, you likely will not be able to use the franchise as collateral because franchisors retain sole rights to award franchises and therefore might not honor any claims against the franchise. If you were to put your business up as collateral and default on the loan, the lender could not take over your franchise, so it would be useless as collateral.

If you are considering the purchase of a franchise, the law requires the franchisor provide you with a detailed report explaining every aspect of the business. This is a requirement of the Federal Trade Commission (FTC), which advises all prospective franchisees to carefully read these reports. A meticulous review will protect yourself and your investment. Employ a lawyer or CPA who is aware of FTC regulations to double-check these documents for potential problems. These two professionals can save you from getting into trouble and losing money.

One more option many startup companies have used, especially in the past, is credit cards. If you have good personal credit and a high enough limit, you might be able to borrow the money from yourself. Be wary of high interest rates, and be sure you will be able to pay the monthly fees. Talk to your accountant and your banker about loan details. If you lend money to your company, you might be entitled to interest on the loan and repayment.

B

List of Resources

Associations

American Staffing Association, **www.americanstaffing.net**, offers members several benefits, including educational and networking opportunities. The website also provides industry news, staffing industry statistics, and educational articles.

National Association of Personnel Services, **www.recruitinglife.com**, focuses its efforts primarily on educating staffing professionals. The organization offers its members an annual conference, certification program, e-learning opportunities, and continuing education initiatives.

National Association of Professional Employer Organizations, **www.napeo.org**, touts itself as the largest professional organization for the staffing industry. In addition to its educational initiatives, NAPEO also offers networking and referral opportunities, marketing support, and resources to its members.

National Association of Executive Recruiters, **www.naer.org**, offers staffing professionals focused on executive recruiting information, professional development, and management counsel on running a business and working in the industry.

Government Agencies

U.S. Census Bureau, **www.census.gov**, provides demographic information on the entire United States and regions and other individual segments of the market.

Small Business Administration (SBA), **www.sba.gov**, provides information, resources, and more to support small business operations throughout the U.S.

SCORE, **www.score.org**, is a partner of the SBA in helping small business owners and entrepreneurs effectively and efficiently run their businesses.

Staffing Franchises

Interim HealthCare, **www.interimhealthcare.com/franchise**, offers an opportunity for opening a staffing service for workers in the health care industry.

Personalized Management Associates, **www.pmafranchise.com**, provides franchise opportunities for those looking to specialize in the restaurant, retail, and hospitality industries.

Apogee, **www.franchisegator.com/Apogee-opportunity**, provides a franchise opportunity for those looking to open and operate an executive search and recruiting business.

American Recruiters, **www.americanrecruiters.com**, provides opportunities for opening and running a health care recruiting business.

At Work Personnel, **www.atworkpersonnel.com**, allows operation of a temporary, temp-to-hire, payroll, and full-time placement service.

Web Resources

www.craigslist.org, free classified ad service online for posting ads and finding candidates.

www.careerbuilder.com, an online job bank for finding candidates.

www.monster.com, an online job bank for finding candidates.

www.6figurejobs.com, a free database of résumés for senior executives.

www.theladders.com, a website devoted to finding candidates and placing job posts for career positions that pay at least six figures.

Books

101 Strategies for Recruiting Success, Where, When, and How to Find the Right People Every Time, Christopher W. Pritchard, American Management Association, 1601 Broadway, New York, NY 10019.

Billing Power! The Recruiter's Guide to Peak Performance, Bill Radin, Innovative Consulting.

Poor Richard's Internet Recruiting, Barbara Ling, Top Floor Publishing, **www.topfloor.com**.

Interviewing and Selecting High Performers, Richard H. Beatty, John Wiley & Sons.

Search and Placement! A Handbook for Success, Larry Nobles with Steve Finkel, Placement Marketing Group, P.O. Box 410412, St. Louis, MO 63141, (314) 991-3177, **www.larrynobles.com**.

Glossary

Acceptance: When the employer and candidate agree on the terms and conditions of the position offer.

Applicant: An individual applying for an open temporary or permanent job position.

Assignment: The time period a temporary worker is assigned to fill a specific role or complete a task.

Background check: An investigation of the candidate to ensure they do not have any criminal problems or other problems or issues. This includes checking references and talking with past employers and co-workers. It also entails reviewing financial backgrounds and any other problems the individual might have.

Billing rate: The amount the staffing service charges the client for placing the employee at the client's company.

Candidate: An individual an employer might wish to hire because he or she has the skills and experience the employer seeks.

Client: The employer paying the staffing service to find the candidate.

Contingency: A fee arrangement between the staffing agency and the client in which the staffing service is not paid until the client hires a candidate that the service has sent.

Conversion fee/rate: The fee a staffing service charges a client when the client hires a temporary employee on a permanent basis.

Counteroffer: A current employer offers more money, benefits, or incentives to try to retain an employee who has accepted an employment offer from a client.

Invoice: A bill that is sent to the client to pay for the staffing services provided by the agency.

Offer: The start date and salary or wages the employer offers the candidate.

Pay rate: The fee or rate the staffing service pays the employee. This is most prominently used for temporary agencies at which the employees are employees of the temp agency but are working at a client's location.

Payroll: The wages and salaries paid to employees.

Permanent placement: When the staffing service places an employee to work for a company on a permanent basis.

Placement: When an employer makes an offer to a candidate through the staffing firm, which the candidate accepts. The staffing representative

then works to complete the agreement with documents.

References: Personal and professional contacts candidates provide to the staffing service for speaking with about their past work performance and situation.

Retainer: Fee arrangement between the staffing firm and the client for which the client pays up front for the firm to seek candidates.

Temp-to-perm: This is an employee who is working for a client on a temporary basis with the opportunity to go permanent.

Temporary employee: This is a candidate who works for a company for set period of time or to complete a specific project for a client.

Time sheet: A form the employee completes to describe work hours to submit to the temp agency or staffing service so the he or she receives their paycheck.

Work order: A request that a staffing agency receives from an employer to find the candidate they are looking to fill.

Bibliography

Thurman, Courtney and Entrepreneur Press. *Start Your Own Executive Recruiting Service: Your Step-by-Step Guide to Success.* 2nd ed. 2007.

Cawley, Charissa. *The Complete Guide to Owning and Operating a Home-Based Recruiting Business.* Lincoln: iUniverse.com Inc. 2001.

Pritchard, Christopher. *101 Strategies for Recruiting Success.* New York: AMACOM. 2007.

Thoren Turner, Krista; Breznickm Alan; Adelson, Rachel; Entrepreneur Press. *Start Your Own Staffing Service; Your Step-by-Step Guide to Success.* 2004.

About the Author

Kristie Lorette

A copywriter and marketing consultant, Kristie Lorette is passionate about helping entrepreneurs and businesses create copy and marketing pieces that sizzle, motivate, and sell. It was through her more than 14 years of experience working in various roles of marketing, financial services, real estate, and event planning that Lorette developed her widespread expertise in advanced business and marketing strategies and communications. Lorette earned a  bachelor's in marketing and a bachelor's in multinational business from Florida State University and her MBA from Nova Southeastern University.

Index